ECUMENE: GLOBAL INTERFACE IN AMERICAN CERAMICS

Presented by the National Council on Education for the Ceramic Arts in cooperation with the School of Arts and Design, Visual Arts Gallery at Santa Fe Community College, Santa Fe, New Mexico.

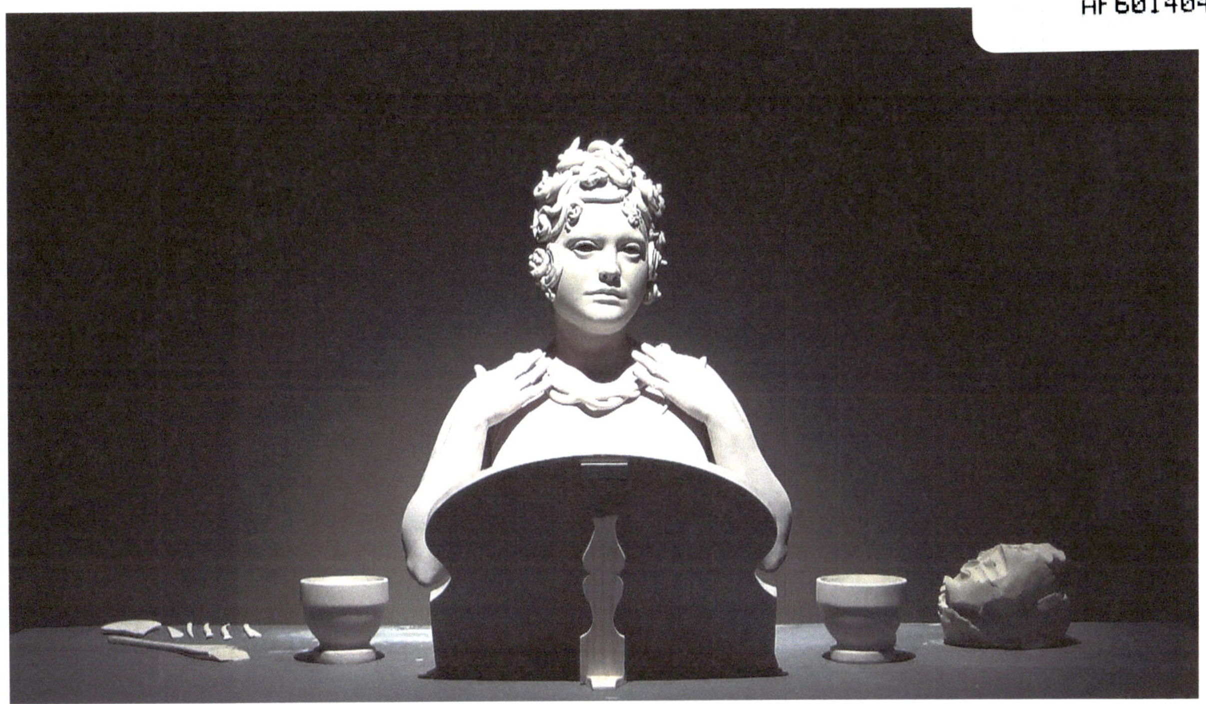

Above: Teri Frame, *PPI: Act III, Hybrids*, 2011, Still from video with raw clay mask

Cover: Andrew Martin, *Kimono*, 2012, Porcelain, 11.5 x 13 x 6.5 Inches

ISBN: 978-1-935046-52-3

ECUMENE: NCECA EXHIBITIONS DIRECTOR'S STATEMENT

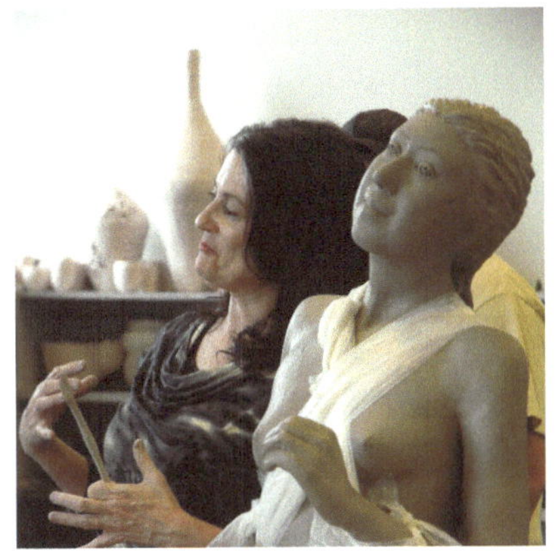

When the International Academy of Ceramics determined to conduct their 2012 General Assembly in Santa Fe, New Mexico, United States of America, its leadership asked the National Council on Education for the Ceramic Arts (NCECA) to provide an exhibition of contemporary American ceramics organized around the meeting's theme of the *New World: Timeless Visions.* After the approval of NCECA's Board of Directors and negotiations with Santa Fe Community College's Visual Arts Gallery, James Marshall, SFCC Ceramics instructor and I developed a theme and the call for submission.

New World conjured images of European explorers landing in what they considered a new world over 500 years ago, where they discovered cultures with long histories of creating ceramic objects of deep cultural meaning, use and beauty. Utilizing knowledge passed down through generations, contemporary indigenous ceramic production in the American Southwest ties into these historic traditions with their respect for materials, processes and styles. Bernard Leach, in his search for the taproot of American ceramics championed this indigenous tradition as key to understanding American ceramics, but came to the realization that the cultural traditions brought to America by immigrants added essential ingredients to the mix. Since the mid-20th century, communication and information technology have expanded dramatically offering access to huge amounts of information about historical styles and processes. Higher education has embraced ceramic history and included their understanding to art history courses and studio programs. Global travel is affordable and convenient, allowing artists personal experiences in cultures far different from their own. This access to information, traditions and cultures previously available to only those born into a tradition have indeed opened the doors to a new world, the entire world inhabited by man.

This new world, the Ecumene, is vast, inclusive and universal.

Faced with the enigma of how to make sense of it and find their place within its wide boundaries, some artists limit themselves to their geographic locations and its cultural traditions but many artists are selecting elements, processes, materials and styles from diverse influences and combining them to create unique, personal statements that reflect their engagement of a broader knowledge and involvement in the global community. Crossing boundaries between the spheres of art, craft, design and entertainment, the artists' work included in *Ecumene: Global Interface in American Ceramics* reflects the richness and complexity of contemporary American ceramic practice within the context of global culture.

Linda Ganstrom
NCECA Exhibitions Director

Linda Ganstrom, NCECA Exhibitions Director served in the roles of director and juror for ***Ecumene: Global Interface in American Ceramics****. Avidly curious about the role of ceramics in cultures past, present and future, Linda has traveled through reading, research and in person to China, Mexico and Europe. A Professor of Art and Design at Fort Hays State University for nearly two decades, Linda enjoys a life rich and full of family, teaching, studio and service. As NCECA Exhibitions Director since 2008, she has directed two* ***NCECA Biennials****, regional exhibitions* ***Continental Divide*** *and* ***Uncommon Ground****, and curated* ***Push Play*** *and* ***Earth Matters****,* ***NCECA Invitationals****.*

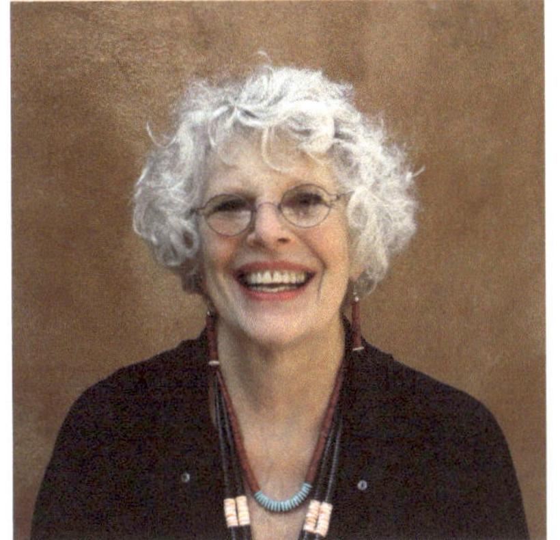

I would like to thank NCECA for inviting me to be a juror for *Ecumene: Global Interface in American Ceramics*. It was an honor to view the large number of images submitted by many artists in various stages of their career. I also want to thank Linda Ganstrom for setting the stage for a very fair jury process, Santa Fe Community College and Clark Baughan for providing excellent technical assistance in addition to being a juror, and fellow juror James Marshall who lead many interesting conversations and attempted to keep us on track given the time constraint.

My prevailing thoughts about the process and the final show selection focus on the enormous task of selecting the final pieces to be in the exhibition. There were so many outstanding choices that it was exceedingly difficult to narrow the selection to the optimal number of art works for the gallery at SFCC. There were numerous additional pieces that I wanted to select if only there was space. In a few instances we selected 2 pieces by the same artist but only because they were small and the second piece was needed to support the artist's intention. The most labored and difficult decisions came at the end and took several hours to complete. I never remember feeling such angst over removing a selection in favor of another one.

Understanding and incorporation of the show title "Ecumene" was not always clear to see in the work. The jurors worked hard to use an open interpretation but did eliminate a few pieces because the connection was not present in our minds.The admissions were varied and offered an expansive view of American ceramics from a traditional teapot to an installation and video piece. I felt that a number of artists are working in an extraordinary scale. Many of the pieces submitted demonstrated grasp of important concepts and excellent technical skills in the use of clay. There were several surprising uses of clay in the submissions. The jurors agreed on the inclusion of small works as well as large ones. We all sought a balance of new ideas, traditional methods and subject matter and agreed that we wanted an exhibit that would speak to a broad audience.

Jane Sauer
Juror

MEET THE JURORS: JANE SAUER

Owner of the Jane Sauer Gallery, Jane is nationally recognized for her commitment to material-based art. Her involvement includes curating numerous exhibits for art centers, universities, and museums. She has juried over 26 exhibitions in the United States, Australia and Japan. Before owning Jane Sauer Gallery, Jane was a studio artist for over 35 years. Her work is in the collection of over 22 museums in the United States, Japan, China, Switzerland, and Norway. Jane has been an active advocate for the arts since receiving a BFA and MA from Washington University. She has served on numerous boards and was President of the American Craft Council from 1995-97. She is included in the Archives of American Art and Smithsonian Institute of American Art, Washington, D.C. Jane received two National Endowment for the Arts Visual Arts Grants, a Distinguished Alumni Award from Washington University, and currently serves on the Advisory Board for Washington University School of Art and Santa Fe University of Art and Design.

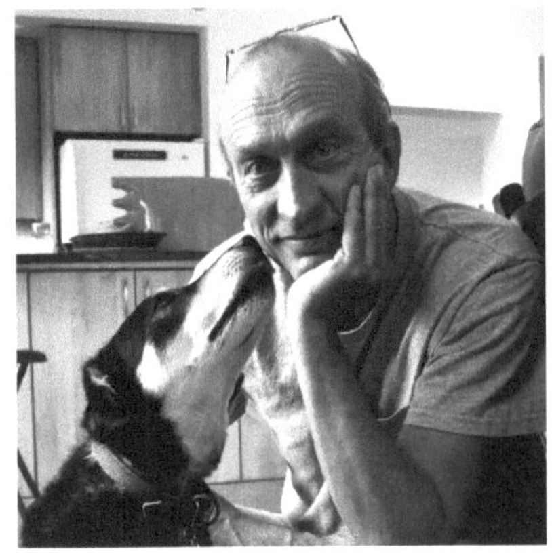

In jurying for *Ecumene: Global Interface in American Ceramics,* I sought to support work representing the versatility, heritage, and contemporary nature of clay. I have always responded to the breadth of ceramics; which represents a continuity from our earliest cultures. The ceramic arts are also uniquely capable of expressing observations and concepts specific to our time.

The jurors deliberated the theme of Ecumene throughout the selection process. We are in a time of instantaneous communication and the corresponding saturation of image, idea and market. Finding an 'ecumenical' perspective (defined as worldwide or general in extent, influence or application) within this context has become more readily possible through global communication.

Art is, I believe, an essential component in maintaining and expressing our very humanity. With every commodity now seemingly available for purchase, there is a grounding and spiritual reality involved in simply 'making'. This creative act avails the logos by realizing the voice within ourselves; reaffirming our humanity.

Clark Baughan
Juror

Clark Baughan is Director of Exhibitions for Santa Fe Community College's Visual Arts Gallery and Red Dot Gallery, a student run commercial venue. He has been with SFCC since 2000 and was instrumental in the foundational development of the SFCC Department of Fine and Performing Arts, developing course work in several areas of studio art as well as portfolio, internship and gallery studies. Under his direction the Visual Arts Gallery has developed into a respected academic venue, featuring numerous curated group exhibitions of national, international and Northern New Mexico artists.

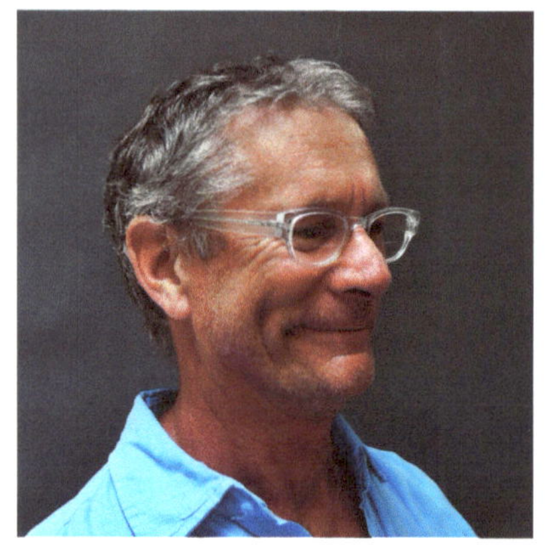

Imagine yourself transported into a room where 31 different languages are being spoken simultaneously and no translator is available to decipher what is being said.

Over there a re-chromed post-apocalyptic shopping cart is filled with strange and shiny bulbous forms. Clearly not something you would experience while grocery shopping at your local market.

Close by an English inspired teapot, covered in computer generated graphic surface design, is observing a dog that is frantically running away from a Shishi, or Chinese stone lion. Perhaps that teapot is offering the both of them a spot of tea.

As you turn away, your eyes land upon a Day of the Dead post-apocalyptic figure that is being escorted to a promised after-life by colorful flowers and birds from Tenochtitlan. A very tiny, yet quite intrepid and fearless mouse sits quietly nearby witnessing that Dead figure's safe arrival to the hereafter.

Now imagine a myriad of unlikely characters, like the above, in one room having multiple conversations about trans-global communication, tribal rituals, and what each may be having for dinner that evening.

Each is speaking in a different tongue and you are the translator. You, with the confidence of a seasoned artist, approach the jury process for this exhibit with art history firmly under your belt. You have digested a myriad of articles on the subject and you are thinking to yourself that this will be a piece of cake.

But, believe me, deciphering and choosing from over 1000 works of ceramic art those few pieces that are felt appropriate for the theme at hand is no small task. The jurors labored for over 12 hours, deliberating, defending, affirming, and denying which works belong and which do not. Difficult, rather subjective, and challenging though it was, the process was a true privilege to be given the opportunity to "see into" each artist's original voice and make those hard choices.

MEET THE JURORS: JAMES MARHSALL

The works in this exhibit, to a greater or lesser degree, are speaking about the dissolving of cultural and aesthetic boundaries. They speak about the dissolving of these boundaries moving from trans-village to trans-global and in some small way, about this earth and the precious life thread that connects us all. They are, in fact, using the earth itself, as a voice to speak in a language beyond words and cultural boundaries.

It is therefore hoped that the viewer will search and discover, from the works chosen, the original voice that all things have in common. A voice that points to the mystery and wonder of what it means to be a sentient being on this planet.

James Marhsall
Juror

James Marshall received his MFA in 1979 from the University of Michigan, Ann Arbor. For the past 12 years James has been Program Head of Ceramics at Santa Fe Community College, in Santa Fe, New Mexico where he has created and built one of the most successful ceramics programs and facilities, both public and private, in the state.

James has been an exhibiting artist for the past 30 years and has over 250 works in public and private collections. He has been widely published in books, magazine and newspaper articles. His current gallery representation includes Winterowd Fine Art, Santa Fe, NM, William Havu Gallery, Denver, CO, William Campbell Contemporary Art, Ft. Worth, TX, Aberson Projects, Tulsa, OK, and Bentley Galleries, Scottsdale, AZ.

The work I've produced over the years was often influenced by looking at historical Asian references. Inspired by forms and shapes common to Asia, I incorporate various historical references to develop my own forms. I also incorporate slip decoration with my own vision of the contemporary look in the works I am currently making.

Man Ho Cho is originally from Hong Kong, China. He came to the United States to study at Northwest Missouri State University where he graduated with a BA focusing on ceramics. Currently, he is a studio potter.

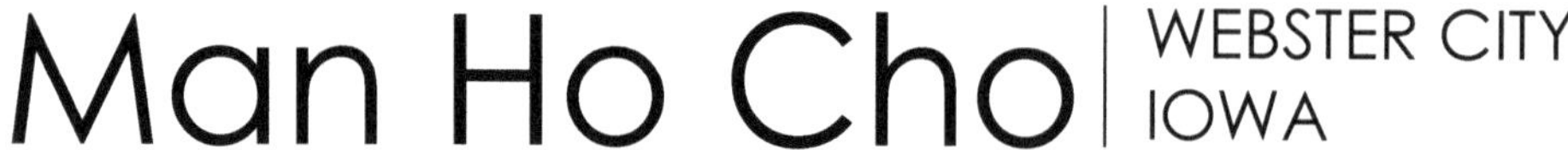

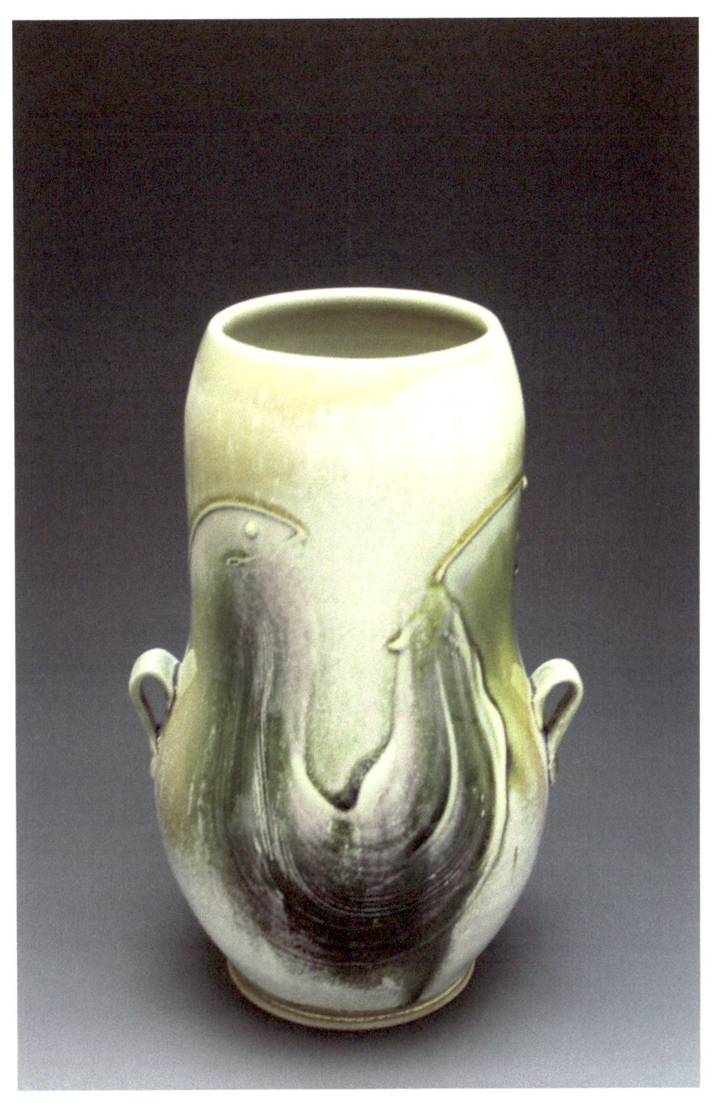

Man Ho Cho
Vase, 2012
White stoneware, slip, sprayed glazes
9 x 6.5 x 6 Inches

My goal in making these pieces has been to create work, which like a good meal, leaves a healthy, full feeling. I am interested in achieving a sense of balance and equanimity in these clay drawings -first of course one must find this within oneself. I am trying to find a place of resolution and stillness in self and in the work: not something without character or animation, but something without dilemma, something content, untroubled and of good cheer.

For me, good work springs from compassion. My "technique" amounts to wishing the work well as it moves through the process of forming, articulation of the surface and firing. I try to find ways of working that respond to the only ability I have ever had, wishing the work well and silently encouraging it to "be good, be good." I keep returning to the studio simply trying to bring as much sincerity as I can muster to bear upon the work.

I am interested in distinguishing the record of the moment when the hand touches clay and the actual quality of feeling surrounding the work. The standard of success I am interested in is one which gauges the work's caliber of compassion and intelligence - the liveliness of its response to being touched by a human. Above all, my works are intended to be good to live with and interact with on a daily basis. If these works have managed to even touch joy, I would be very happy.

Bede Clarke has been a Professor of Art at the University of Missouri since 1992. He received his MFA from the University of Iowa (1990) and a BFA from Eckerd College (1982). Clarke has been working in ceramics for 40 years and maintains a studio in Columbia, Missouri where he produces his work for exhibitions recently at: Red Lodge Clay Center, Red Lodge, MT; Ogden Museum of Southern Art, New Orleans, LA; Crocker Museum of Art Sacramento, CA; Ohio Craft Museum Columbus, OH. Bede's work is in the collections of the Bermuda National Gallery, the Martin Museum of Art, and the Racine Art Museum.

Bede Clarke | COLUMBIA MISSOURI

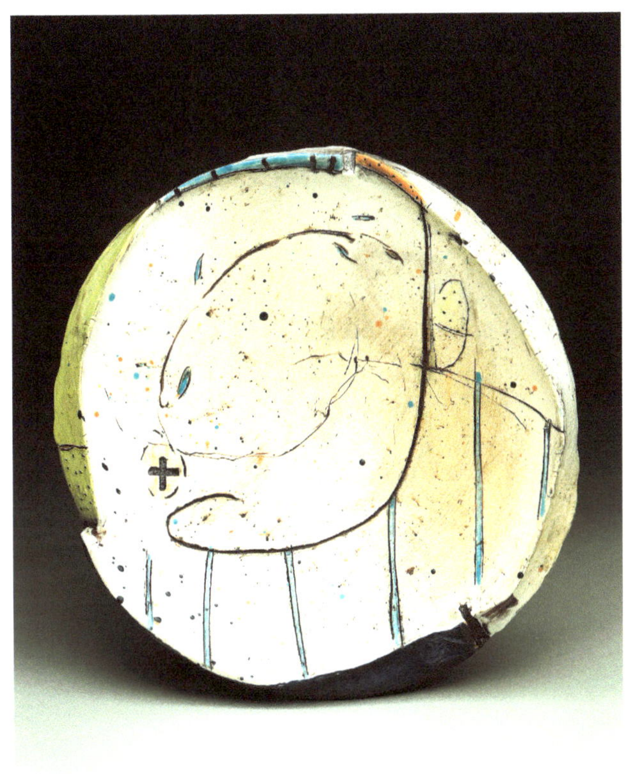

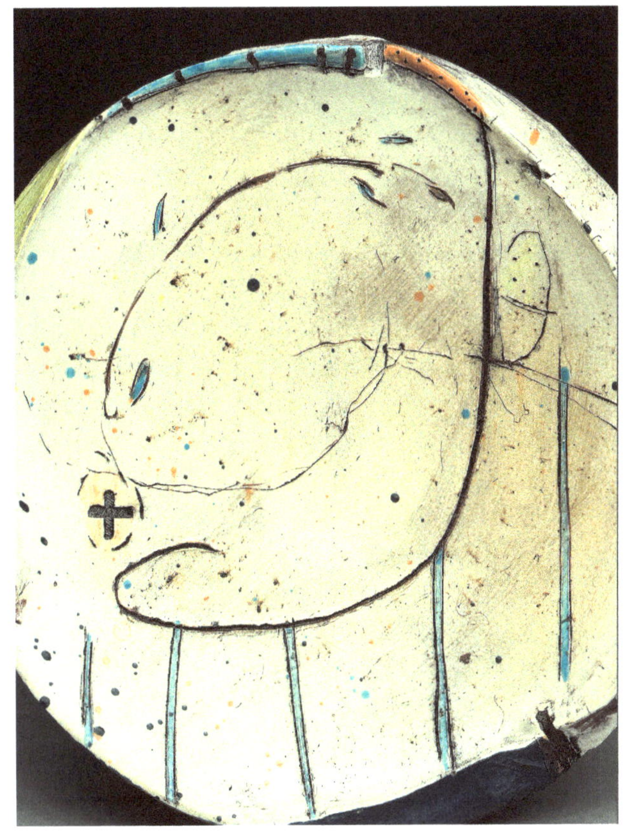

Bede Clarke
Bowl, 2012
Earthenware, polychrome engobes
12 x 12 x 2 Inches

I am passionate about objects. I see them as a point of interaction—a key to understanding a broader context. Whether historical or contemporary, objects are imbued with the story of their making and a purpose in being. I am interested in how an object communicates or how it works as an interface. Why is it able to describe its beginning in the hand of its maker? How does it tell of its origin in the need to perform a specific task? In my work I explore the potential for objects to communicate a breadth of social and cultural origins. The groupings fabricated with such objects create a strange simultaneity in their arbitrary placement skewing the read of an apparently formal composition. Like a pensively delivered observation, a singular moment is created that alludes to expansive notions of origin and purpose.

William DePauw received his BFA in painting from Northern Michigan University in 1996. He began exploring object making with clay that same year. He received his MFA from Tulane University in 2004 concentrating in ceramics. He has held the position of Professor of Practice and Ceramics Lab Tech in the Newcomb Art Department at Tulane University since 2006. He currently lives in New Orleans with his wife Rachael.

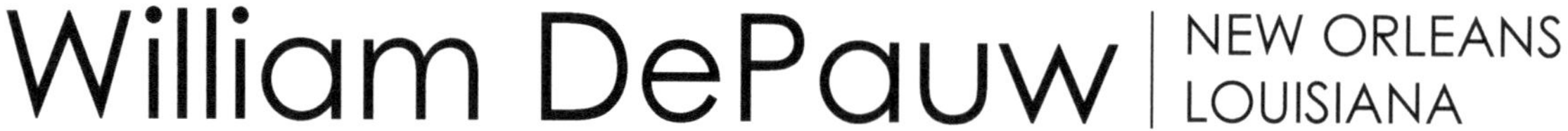

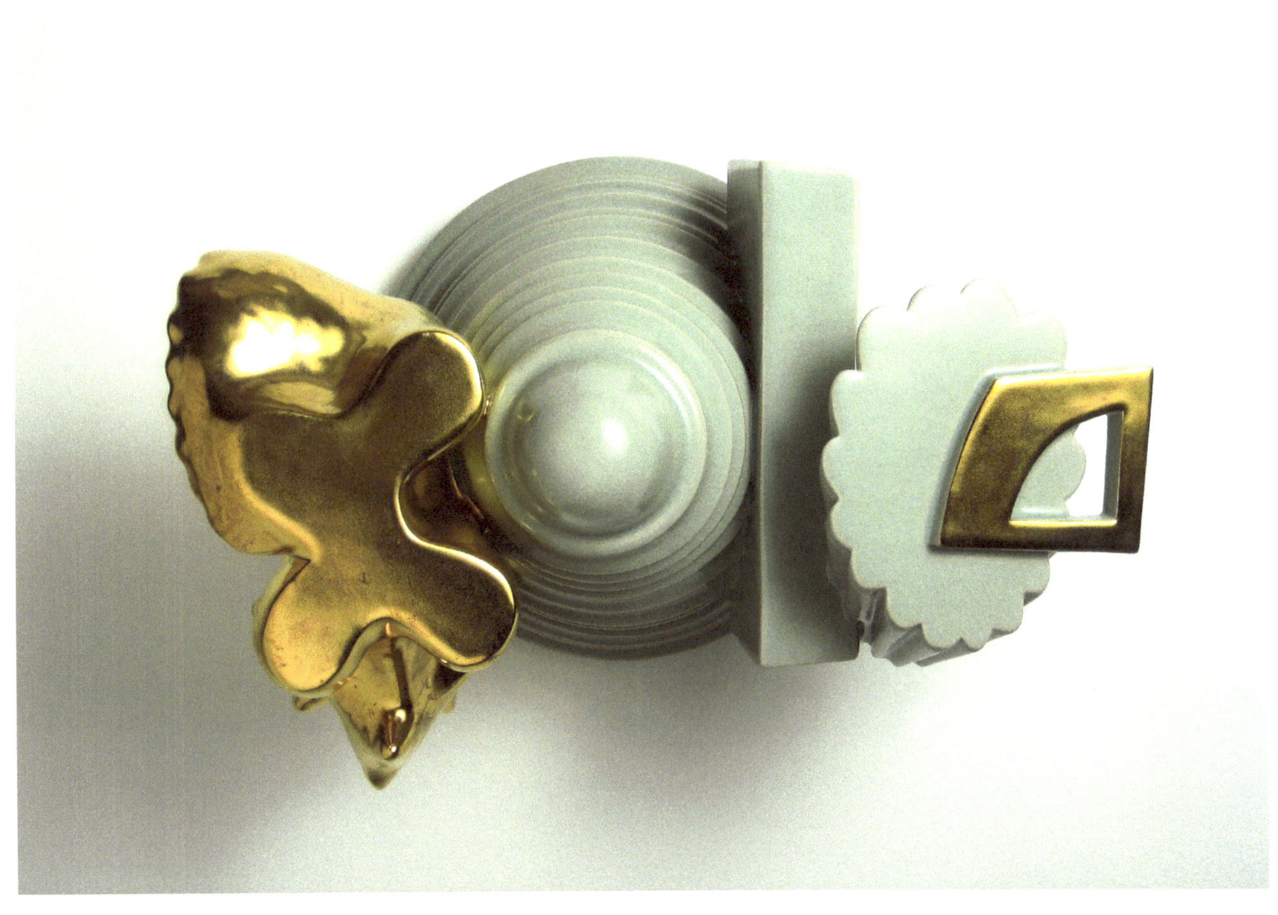

William DePauw
Foundling Rest, 2009
Porcelain, lusters, glaze
10 x 16 x 10

I have recently had the opportunity to travel to Germany and China. The work that I included in this exhibition is a synthesis of two very distinct cultural experiences. With the opportunity to be influenced firsthand by very drastically different ways of working and philosophy of making; I am challenged to determine where I fit within the global standing as an object maker. In recent works, such as Ridge, I present my exploration of what it means to be an object maker in a post-industrial society and explore where handmade utilitarian vessels fit into contemporary life.

Thomas Edwards is currently a graduate student at the University of Nebraska-Lincoln. In 2010 he was awarded the Baden-Württemberg Stipend for Vocationally Qualified People. In 2008 he graduated with honors, receiving his BFA from Tennessee Tech University. Also in 2008 he was awarded the Windgate Fellowship, which he used to travel to Jingdezhen, China.

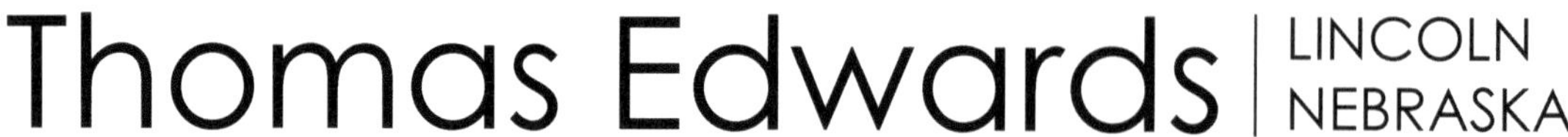

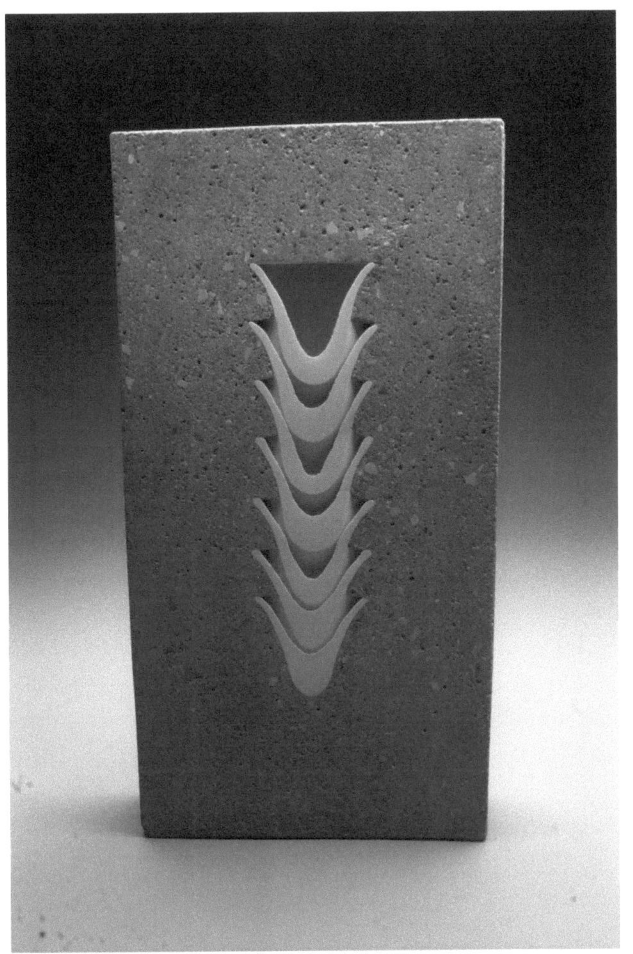

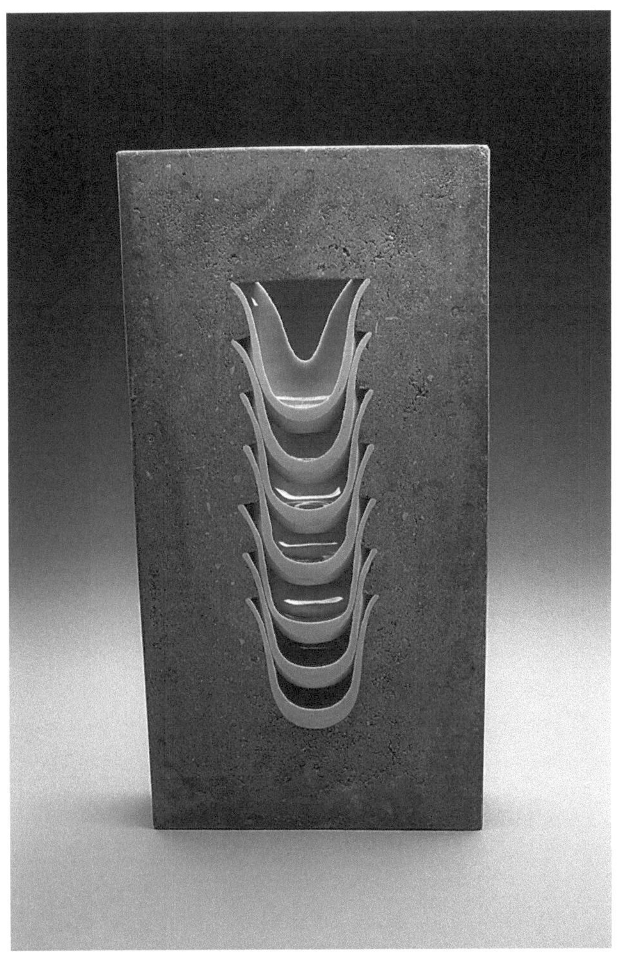

Thomas Edwards
Ridge, 2012
Porcelain, concrete
22.5 x 12 x 3 Inches

I have been traveling the past eight summers to and working in Jingdezhen, the porcelain city of China. My summer home away from home has become an integral part of my personal and professional life. I have now developed a distinct body of work that I could only produce in Jingdezhen from the historic white clay. Having a background in low-fire terra-cotta clay it took the first five years exploring, learning and finding comfort working in porcelain. The sculptural work made the past three years has become an assimilation of my aesthetics into high temperature clay. The pieces are me working and living in China with all the cultural influences around. I have found it a fascinating experience to fully immerse myself in another culture and see what instinctively becomes part of me.

Gary Erickson received his BA degree from Hamline University in St. Paul, Minnesota and his MFA from the New York State College of Ceramics in Alfred, New York. His sculpture and tile work has been shown nationally and internationally. His work is in many private and public collection, including the National Museum of American Art, Renwick Gallery in Washington D.C. He has participated in several international residencies in both Cuba and China. He teaches at Macalester College in St. Paul, Minnesota and maintains a studio in Minneapolis.

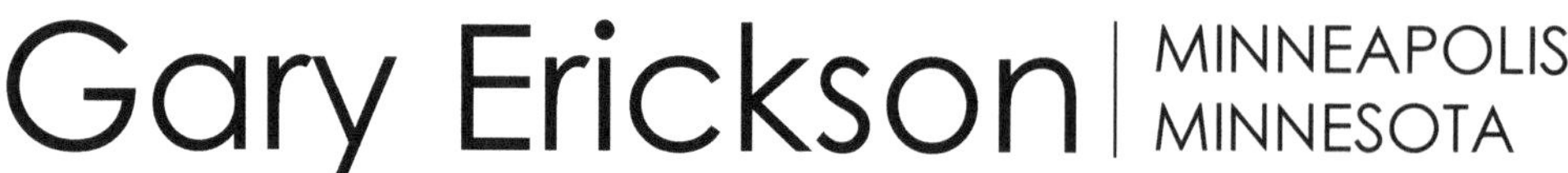

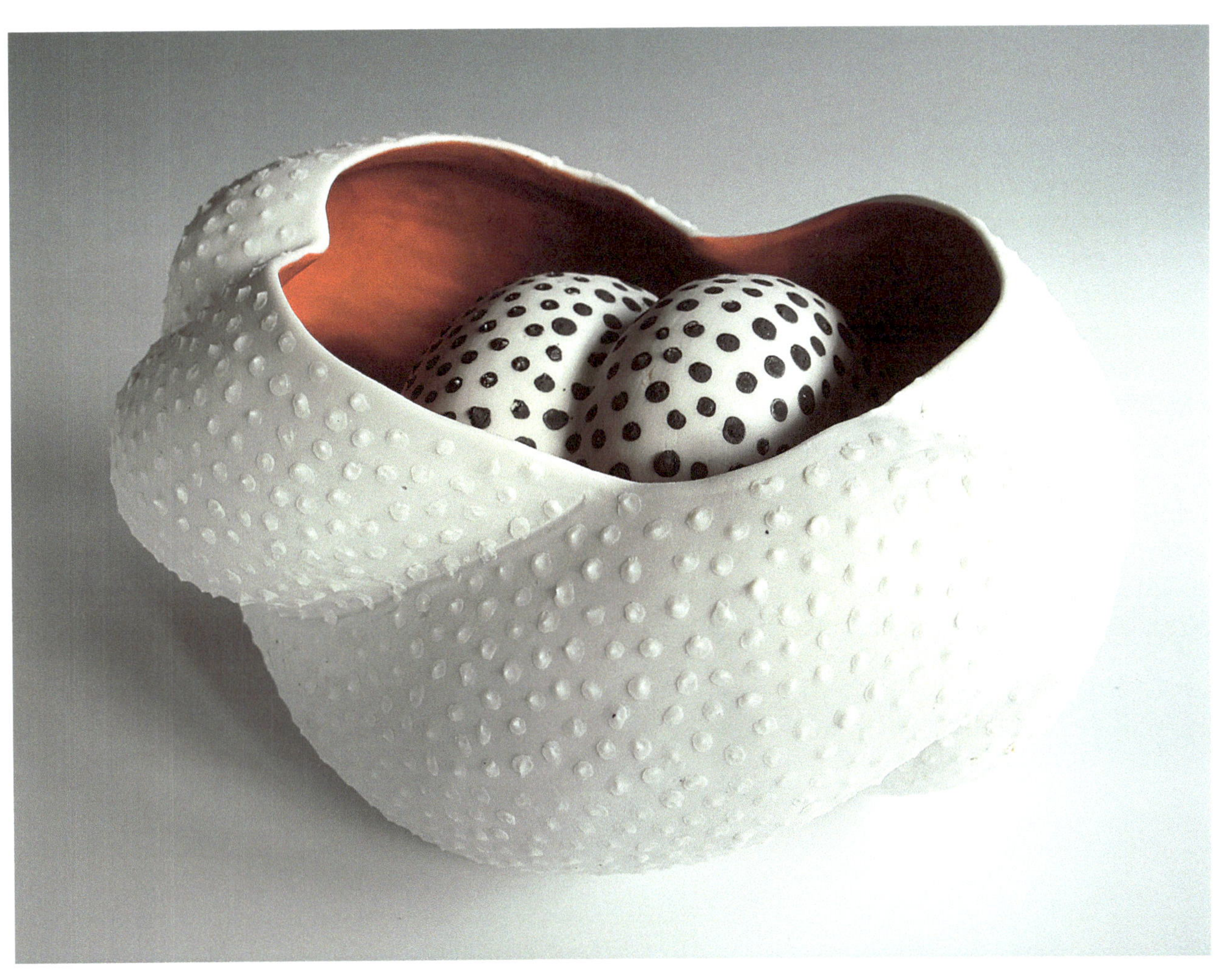

Gary Erickson
Nestled Spiral with Black Dots, 2011
Slip-cast porcelain, underglaze decals, slip washes, unglazed
4 x 7.5 x 5.5 Inches

The idea behind the International ceramics symposium "Porcelain Another Way" was to bring together ceramic artists from all over the world with one thing in common - Porcelain - to interface, design, and exhibit together creating a dialogue of ideas and influence. From the symposium and its participants, I have gained at least 14 different perspectives of contemporary ceramics globally. The work I created during the symposium came about as a result of an experimental design process I was developing in my studio in Kansas City, Missouri previously. I developed a way to create a functional porcelain object whose shape is dictated by things found in the area in which they are created. Incorporating my immediate surroundings into a body of work produces a narrative that speaks of the places my objects were made. It shows similarities and differences within each body of work just as there exists similarities and differences in the actual locations.

Ryan Fletcher is a ceramic artist and designer living and working in Kansas City, Missouri. Fletcher holds a BFA in ceramics from the Kansas City Art Institute and is currently completing a two-year residency at Red Star Studios ending February of 2013. He gains experience from traveling overseas to Eastern and Western Europe seeking influence from various cultures. There, he also gains a broader perspective of the direction of contemporary ceramics and what it means to different communities.

Ryan Fletcher | KANSAS CITY MISSOURI

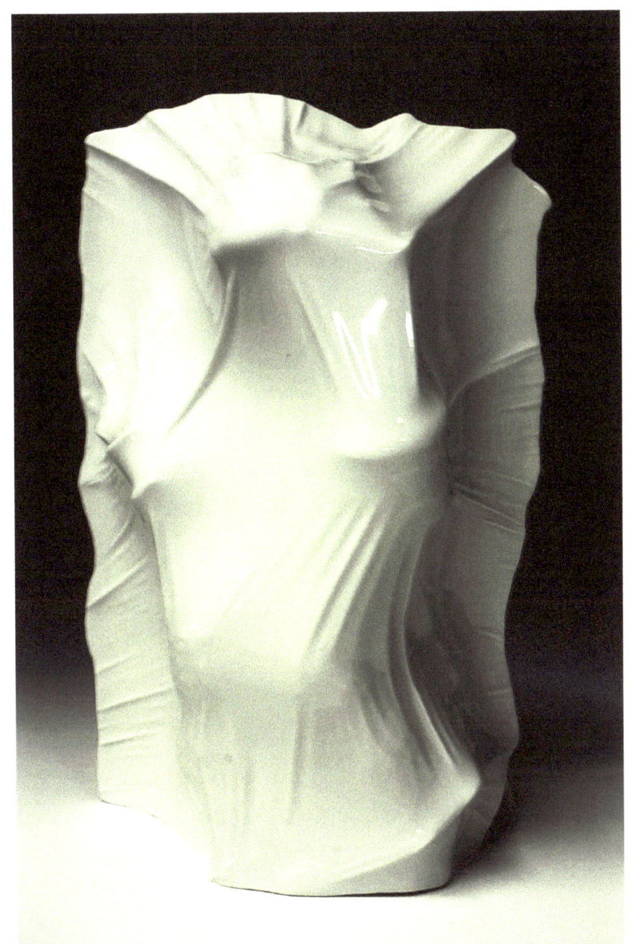
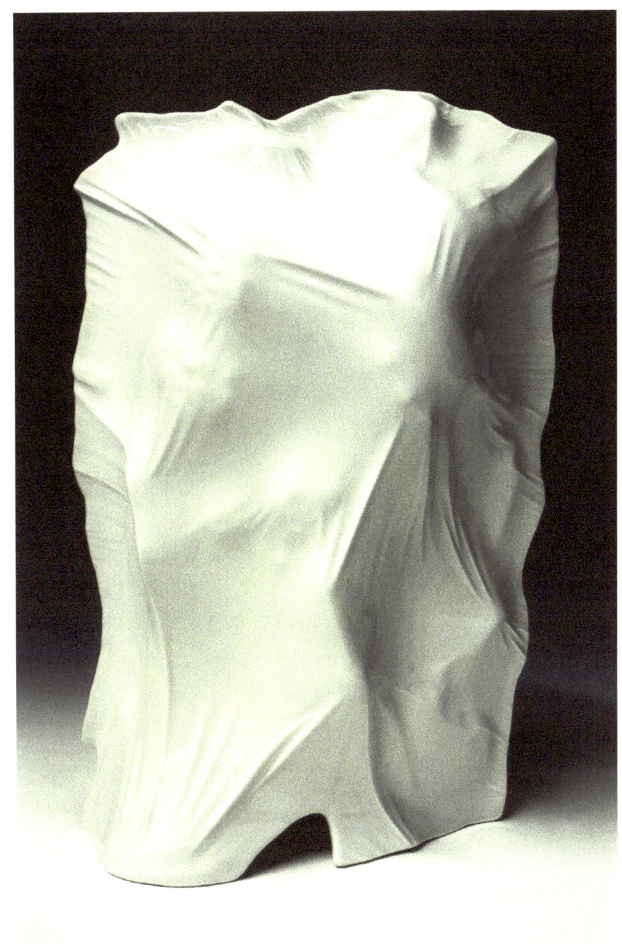

Ryan Fletcher
Pierogi Variation 6, 2011
Porcelain, clear glaze
13 x 7 x 6 Inches
Collection of Dick Belger and Evelyn Craft

The relationship between clay and the human body has been expressed through endless cosmogonies, tribal practices, and three-dimensional representations of the human form. Clay is a material that has been mythically linked with physical embodiment for millennia and across myriads of cultures. It can implicate a hairless, fleshy landscape and emulate the skin's life-glow. As clay dries it takes on the delicately withered patterns of the aging body. The mutable nature of this material allows for a process through which I seek transmutation.

My work is an investigation that juxtaposes anomaly against ideal Western bodily paradigms such as the model of proportion as conveyed in Greek statuary, the Enlightenment concept of purity as reflected within 18th century beauty trends, paragons of the eugenics movement, recent attempts to link the Fibonacci string model with the growth of DNA repetitive sequences, and efforts to apply the golden ratio to the proportions of nucleobases in the human genome. Such topics have been at the forefront of philosophical inquiry for centuries. In this contemporary setting, where aesthetic surgery and genetic manipulation abound, they are of specific relevance.

Teri Frame received a BFA from the Kansas City Art Institute and an MFA from Pennsylvania State University. The relationship between clay and the human body has continuously been the center of her interest and this is made evident in her studio practice and research. Although she was trained as a ceramist, performance art and video have come into her work and she continues to move among these genres. Frame has exhibited, lectured, and taught throughout the United States, Canada, and South Korea. She is currently the Ceramics Teaching Fellow at Northland College in Ashland, Wisconsin.

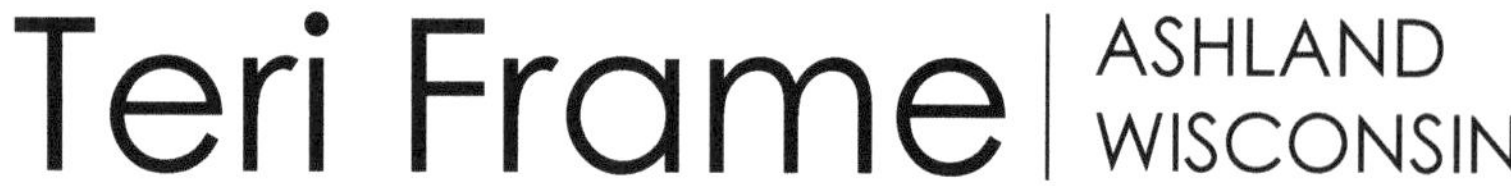

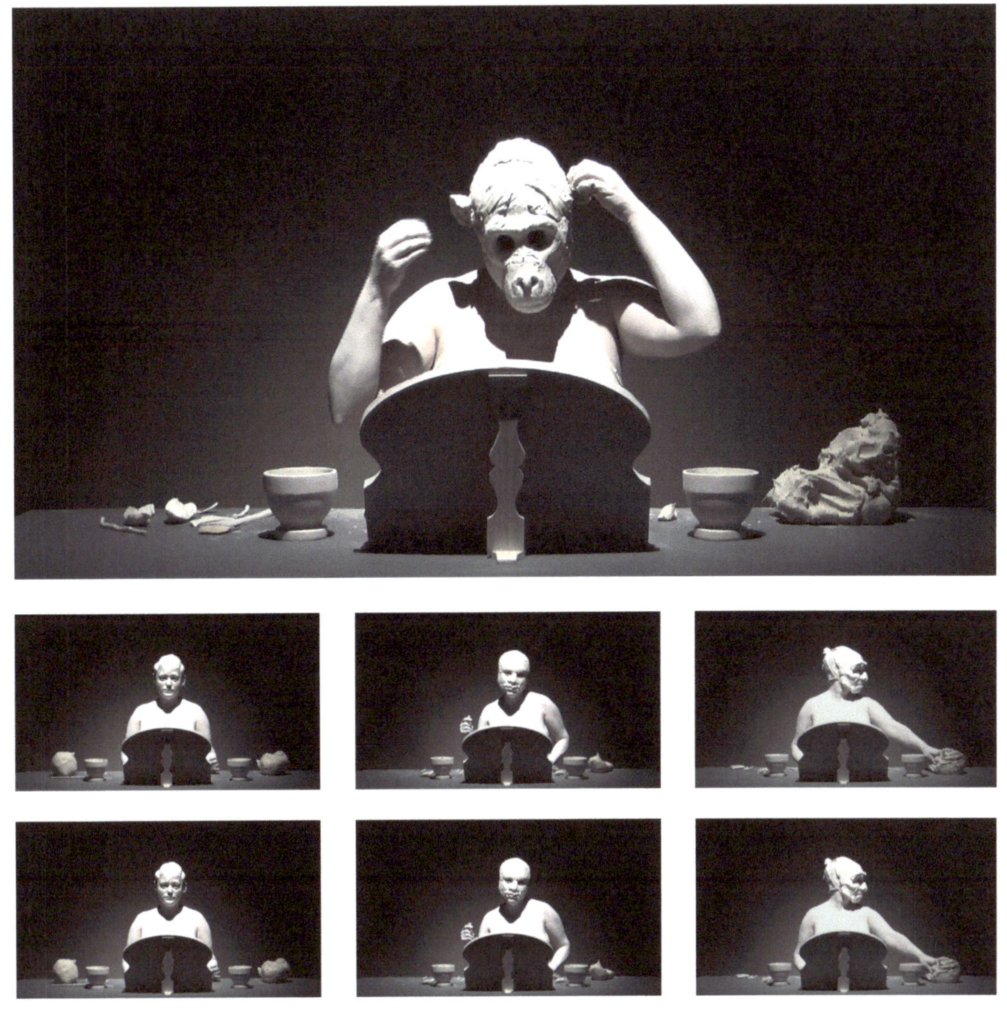

Teri Frame
PPI: Acts I-VI, Simians, Hybrids, Early Humans, Proportions, Races, Post-humans, 2011
Still images from video series, raw clay masks

My work is about creation and destruction, the human struggle for survival and the inevitable end—Death. There are brief, quiet times where my subconscious mingles with and titillates my conscious mind. Enthralled by these moments, various images spring in and out of my brain. I gather some of these images and then assemble them to create clay figures. I am playing with the juxtaposition of biblical creation of man versus the creation of life through genetic engineering. I exploit human mutations and deformities. I hybridize nature's specimens, commenting on the contemporary issues of our genetic future. These characters are generated and simultaneously sacrificed to be displayed in similar manner of ***Cabinet of Curiosities*** *wherein live mutants were regarded as monsters not to be looked at but, in death they are to be displayed and coveted. In my work, I am a mad scientist. In my work, I am playing God.*

Rebeca Gilling was born and raised in Brazil, but now calls Miami, Florida her home. Gilling received her MFA from Miami International University of Art & Design. The inspiration for her ceramic sculptures comes from the *Cabinet of Curiosities* and from man's interference with and modification of animals and humans. She is specifically concerned with capturing the possible results of genetic engineering, cloning and hybridization. Gilling's work has been exhibited in many cities in the U.S. as well as abroad.

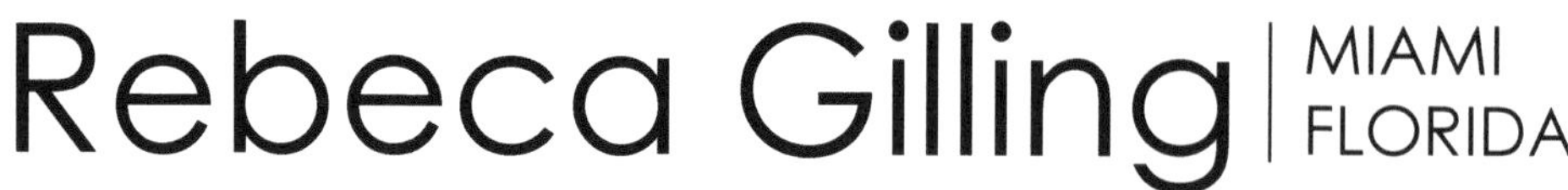

Rebeca Gilling | MIAMI FLORIDA

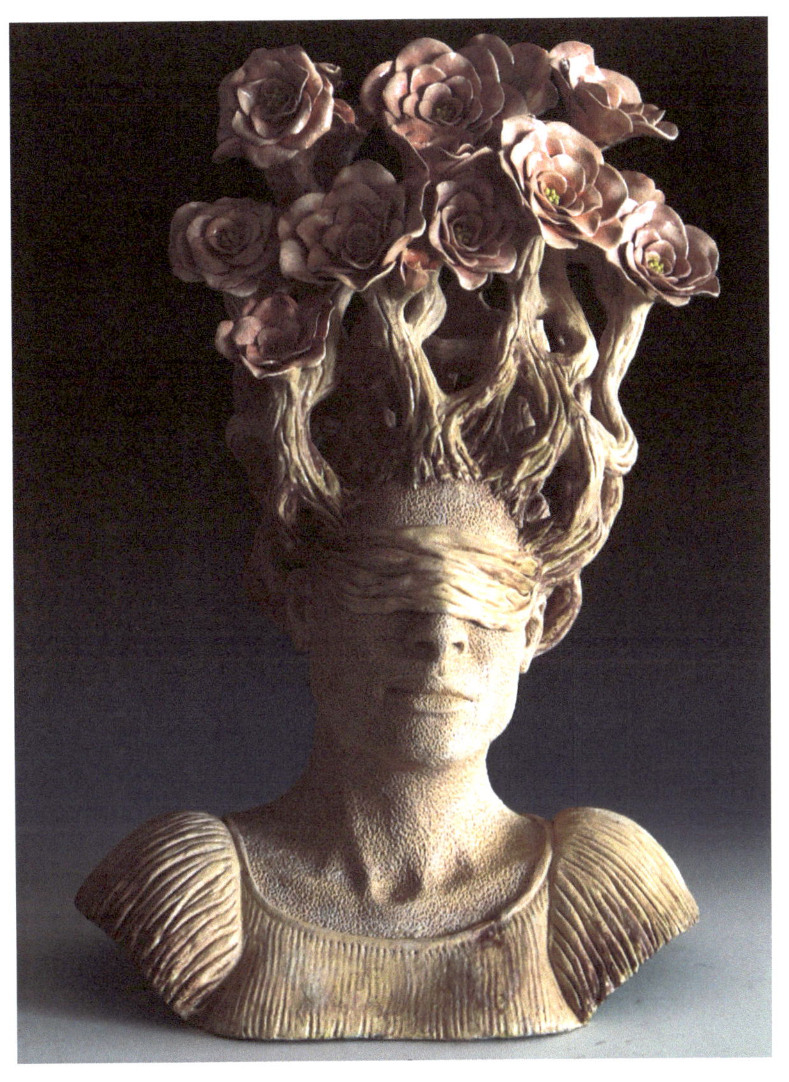

Rebeca Gilling
In the Recesses of Agnes Mind, 2011
Stoneware, underglazes, glaze
24 x 18 x 15 Inches

My art illustrates common threads of the human existence through an exploration of human relationships, sex, power and our place as individuals in a global society. Through the human form my art reveals a world in which the inner psyche of our emotions, fears, beliefs and desires are allowed to emerge. In a world where seven billion people inhabit our planet, we seem to be unable to connect with each other; instead the frantic pace of our lives leaves us feeling more isolated and less fulfilled. We are simply holding on in a world in perpetual motion with little time to look inside ourselves, filter through the endless information and discover what truly makes us human. My work focuses on the commonalities that tie us together; the oftentimes illusory comforts of stability, possessions and relationships. My sculptures illustrate both a celebration of life as well as the vulnerability of the flesh, the idealistic arrogance and vitality of youth juxtaposed with the physical decline and wisdom of age and ultimately the inexorable human pursuit for identity and purpose in contemporary society.

Christine Golden has been creating art for over 15 years, working predominantly with the figure sculpted in clay. She attained her BFA from University of Utah and her MFA from Indiana University in 2010. Golden has participated in numerous workshops and residencies, including Peters Valley Arts and Craft Center, Vermont Studio Center, Watershed Center for Ceramic Arts, Santa Fe Clay, Arrowmont, Penland School of Arts and Crafts, and Red Lodge Clay Studio. She curated an exhibition for NCECA 2012 and will be attending a residency at the LH Project in summer 2012 before becoming the invited artist-in-residence at Northern Arizona University.

Christine Golden | FLAGSTAFF ARIZONA

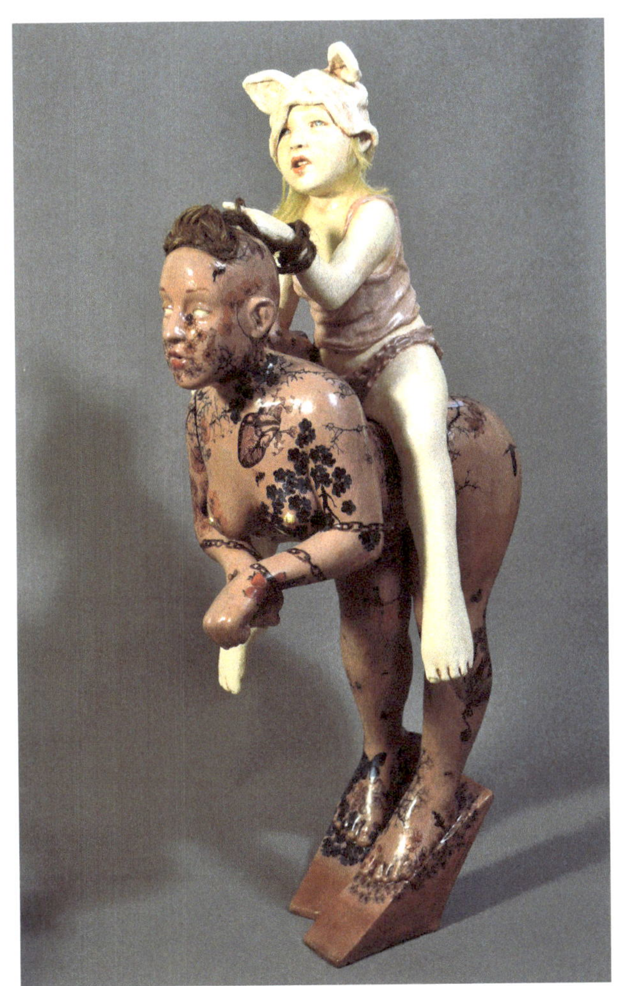

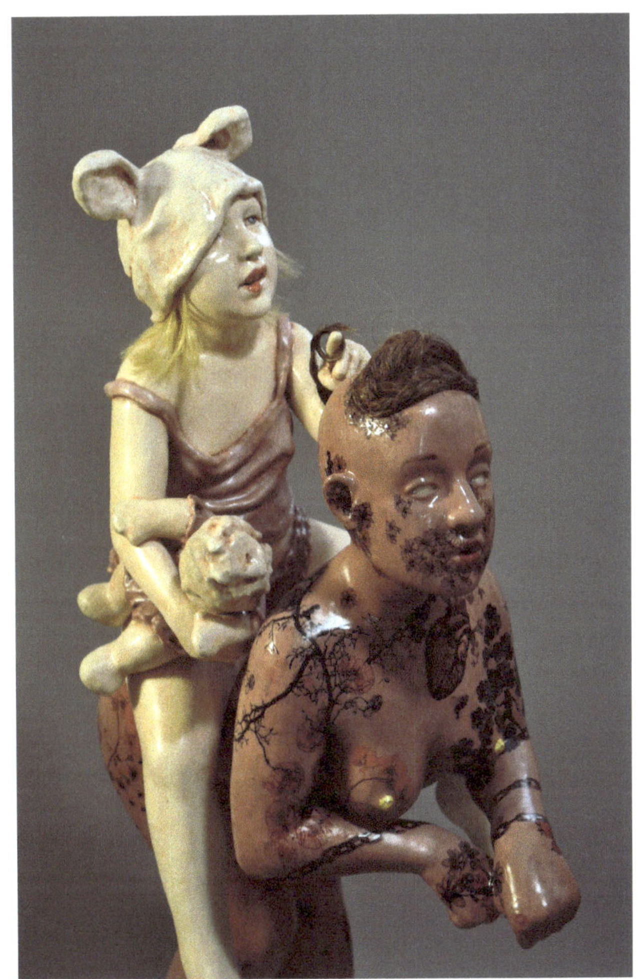

Christine Golden
Jenny's, 2012
Clay, decals, underglaze, slips, oxides, paint, hair
39 x 14.5 x 20 Inches

My influences come partially from the places I grew up-Podunk in Connecticut, and the mountains and lakes of Rangeley, Maine. I was particularly inspired while living abroad by a trip to Lapland in northern Norway. Here, I was astonished and inspired by the ingenuity, practicality, and beauty with which these people made everything they needed. I could not understand why people referred to cultures such as this as primitive. I had not known there were people in the world that still lived this way, and I wanted to learn all about it. As I learned more about cultures of the world, I recognized that this self-reliant lifestyle, close to and with an essential respect for nature, held a strong, intuitive commitment to beauty which was reflected in every part of their daily lives. There was no separation between art and life, the two existed as an integral part of each other. I desired to become a maker of beautiful objects and without really knowing why, at age 14, chose clay as the medium. My imagery is a reflection of 40 years of these observations between animals, myths, ritual, women, families, daily life, world crafts, and the natural world.

The powerful presence of Melissa Greene's pots stems from the way they balance the narrative and the decorative. Some of them describe her past— plants and animals in places she's lived, like the Atlantic coast and the Maine mountains—while others tell of the strength and creativity she sees among women in other cultures. "Listening to stories as a child really activated my imagination."

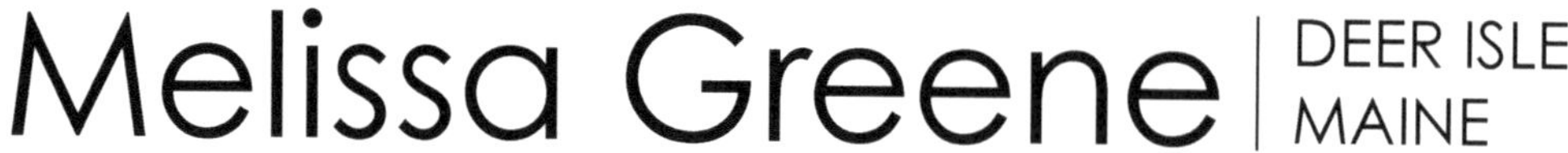

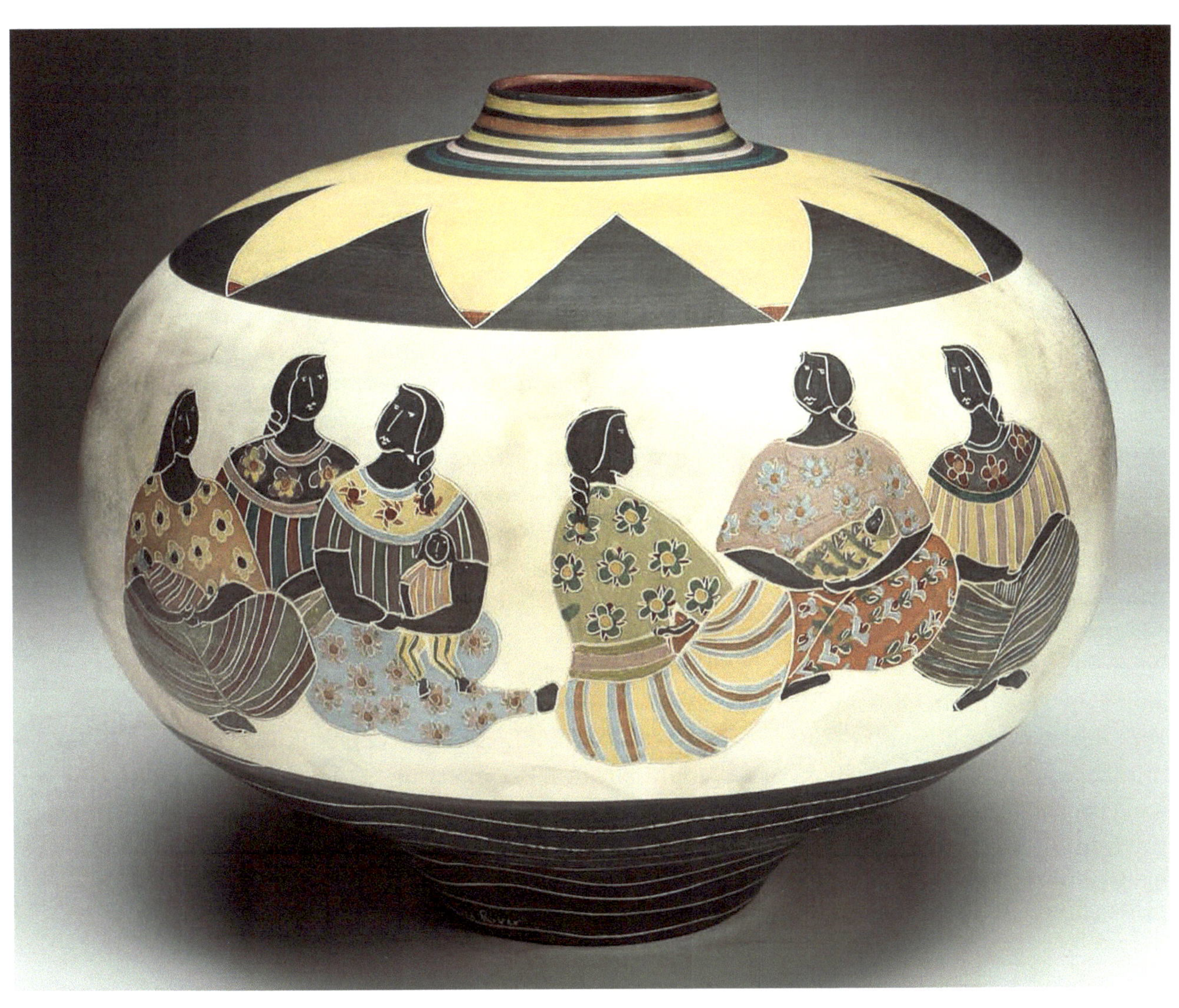

Melissa Greene
Talking by the River, 2012
White earthenware, terra sigillata
13 x 16 x 16 Inches
Photo Ken Woisard

I make coil-built, micaceous clay utilitarian ware and cookware. A couple of the vessels are very Southwestern influenced such as the beanpots and bowls. Many vessels are traditional to other global cultures. My teapots are influenced by Asian teapots and their tea ceremonies. My Central American influenced comals are used by customers to make both tortillas and as a pizza stone for baking. Without the advent of the Internet and immediate access to other cultures I highly doubt I would be making half of the pots in my repertoire. French styled cassoulet dishes are used by customers daily in their kitchens. The conical lidded Moroccan styled tajines have become quite popular with my customers lately. Many customers have no idea what it is but many know exactly what it is and I believe that is due to global influences becoming more and more commonplace in our daily lives.

Over twelve years ago, I started making my first coil-built, micaceous clay beanpots clay. It was also the last time I threw pots on a wheel. Yes, it is a slower technique but one that I felt gave me a much better and exacting control of the clay to create the shapes I wanted for cooking vessels. Long before making my first pots, I spent many, many hours in a kitchen. Now I'm able to combine my love of cooking with a clay that enables me to make cookware designed for daily use in a kitchen.

After four years at DePauw University where he primarily focused on wheel thrown porcelain and stoneware, Brian Grossnickle moved to New Mexico and began a two-year apprenticeship with Jicarilla Apache master potter Felipe Ortega. Grossnickle began coil building cookware from micaceous clay in 2000 and immediately found joy in the connection between maker, material and process of this ancient Southwestern tradition... from harvesting the raw material, to the slow rhythms of coiling the pots, to the proximity of the intense heat from the pit firing. Designed to be used in the kitchen on a daily basis, Grossnickle's cookware has been included in the *Strictly Functional Pottery National* and the Smithsonian Craft Show.

Brian Grossnickle | TIJERAS NEW MEXICO

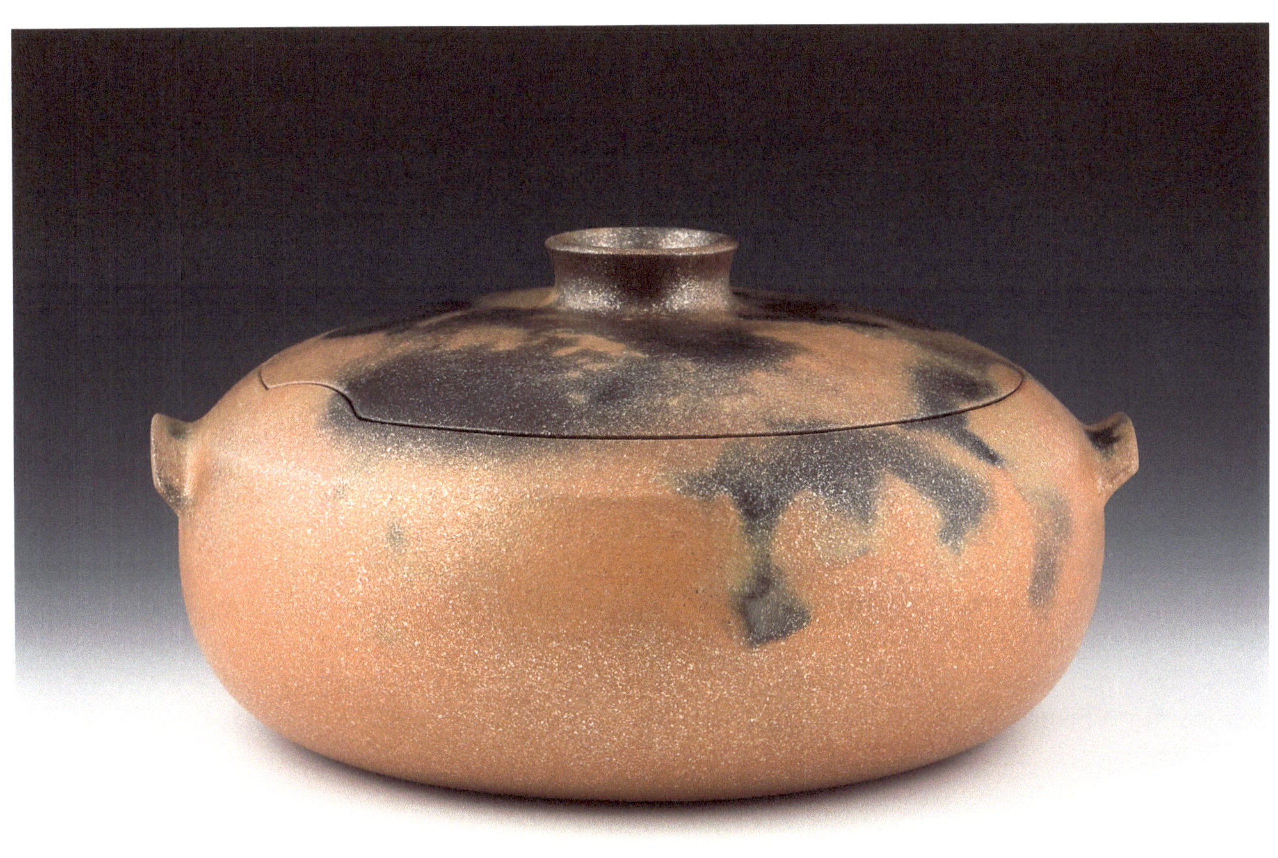

Brian Grossnickle
Casserole 090, 2012
Hand dug micaceous clay
7 x 14 x 15 Inches
Photo Jay Sturdevant

My work examines what I call the domestic identity—how we define ourselves through how we live, where we come from, and the structures we erect and exist within to maintain a sense of security and place. Structure includes actual spaces such as buildings and homes, but also includes relationships, surroundings, and traditions. By expanding our identities to include the global interface, we may confront a new set of anxieties and the potential for a decreased sense of uniqueness. How adhered are we to the notion of nation, culture and tradition? What do we do when those traditions are put into question as part of an ever-expanding, global identity? In my piece Futility (Dog), I present these anxieties through the form of a dog chasing its tail. The compulsion of the dog to chase its tail is, at best, non-productive but also has the potential to be self-destructive. Only from an outside perspective is the futility obvious, as the dog feels the satisfaction in the exploration or the chase. As we continue to expand our identities to include a place in the global culture, we may find ourselves chasing after, not what is new but what is most familiar.

Rebecca Hamlin Green received her MFA in 2012 from the University of Arizona, Tucson, AZ. She is an emerging ceramic installation artist. Her objects and images evoke a strong emotional connection to the home, self-preservation and observation of nature. She often incorporates animal imagery in her work, using the animal form as an analog to human emotion. Drawn particularly to domesticated animals, she relates their experiences alongside and in conjunction to human experiences. Green uses them as metaphorical vehicles through which we first experience the difficult realities of death, birth, loyalty and the power of nature within the domestic space. Hamlin Green is an educator who aims to further her research through institutional teaching opportunities.

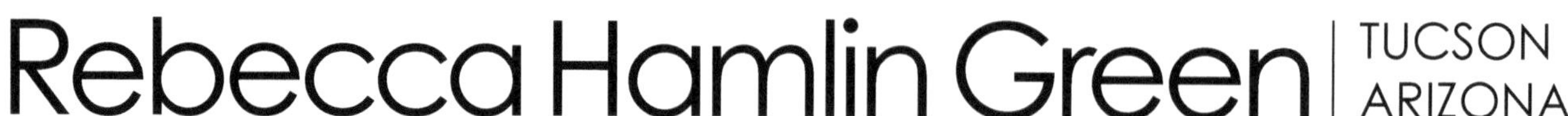

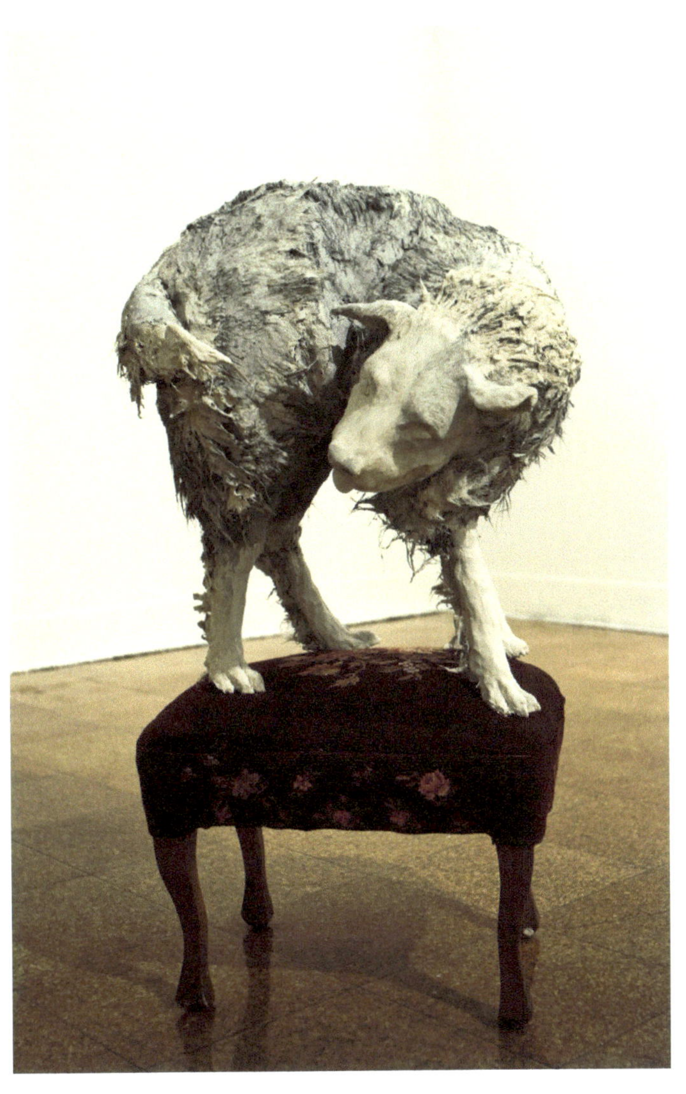

Rebecca Hamlin Green
Futility (Dog), 2012
Fired and unfired porcelain paper clay,
found object
40 x 32 x 20 Inches

As a ceramic artist I have the privilege of traveling the world making connections within a community of artists sharing techniques and ideas. While learning from each culture I'm inspired by the natural environment of each country. I'm utilizing botanical imagery in a biomorphic format to make connections between humanity, environment, beauty and sexuality.

CJ Jilek received her MFA degree from Utah State University during which time she studied in Australia, Korea, China, and Poland. Jilek's ceramic work is as varied as her studies. She creates porcelain biomorphic sculptures fired in oxidation with an atomic color pallet and mixed media elements. Her vessel forms contrast organic and mechanical surfaces finished in subtle atmospheric processes. Jilek is currently looking to explore other corners of the world.

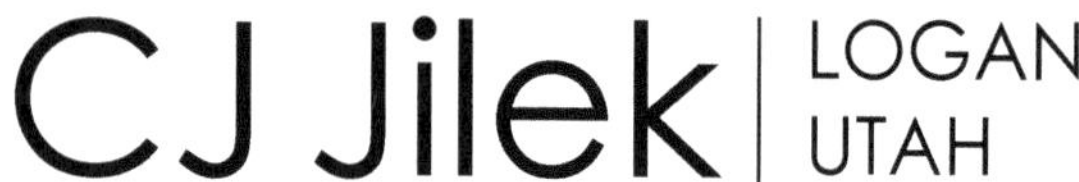

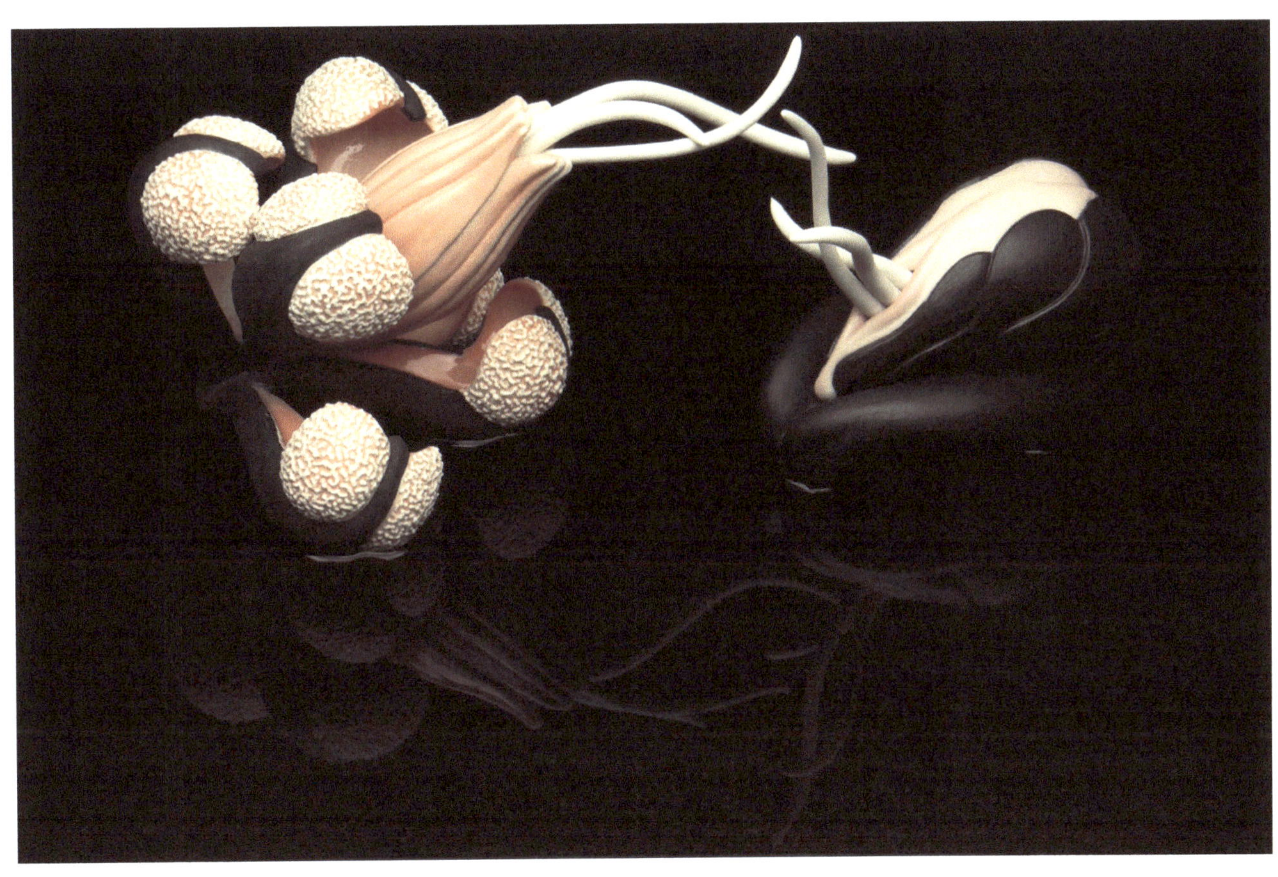

CJ Jilek
Cross Pollination 7, 2011
Slip-cast porcelain, underglaze, glaze, water, metal
7 x 14 x 14 Inches

My work addresses this exhibition's theme through its connection to ceramic history in contrast with its engagement with our technology-driven culture. The themes of artifact and invention have been a consistent exploration of my artwork over the last ten years. I am intrigued by the historical prevalence of clay, a material so strongly linked to our cultural formation. The material is imbued with a sense of time, carrying with it references to the many clay objects created by past civilizations. This rich history seems to be connected to the primal act of making itself. My process of working attempts to support the exploration of time I want my work to reflect. I engage with our technology-driven and computer facilitated culture by designing my pieces on a computer, while building them in an intentionally low-tech way, as a means of keeping them rooted in past traditions of making. Ultimately the pieces I make read as components of a larger whole. They reference ambiguous fragments selected as treasures from a bone yard of a distant tradition.

Peter Christian Johnson currently lives and works in La Grande, Oregon where he is an Associate Professor of Art at Eastern Oregon University. He earned his MFA from Pennsylvania State University and a BS in Environmental Science at Wheaton College. Peter Christian Johnson has been a resident artist or visiting lecturer at the Alberta College of Art and Design, Australian National University, The LH Project, The Archie Bray Foundation, and the Odyssey Center for Ceramic Arts.

Peter Christian Johnson | LA GRANDE OREGON

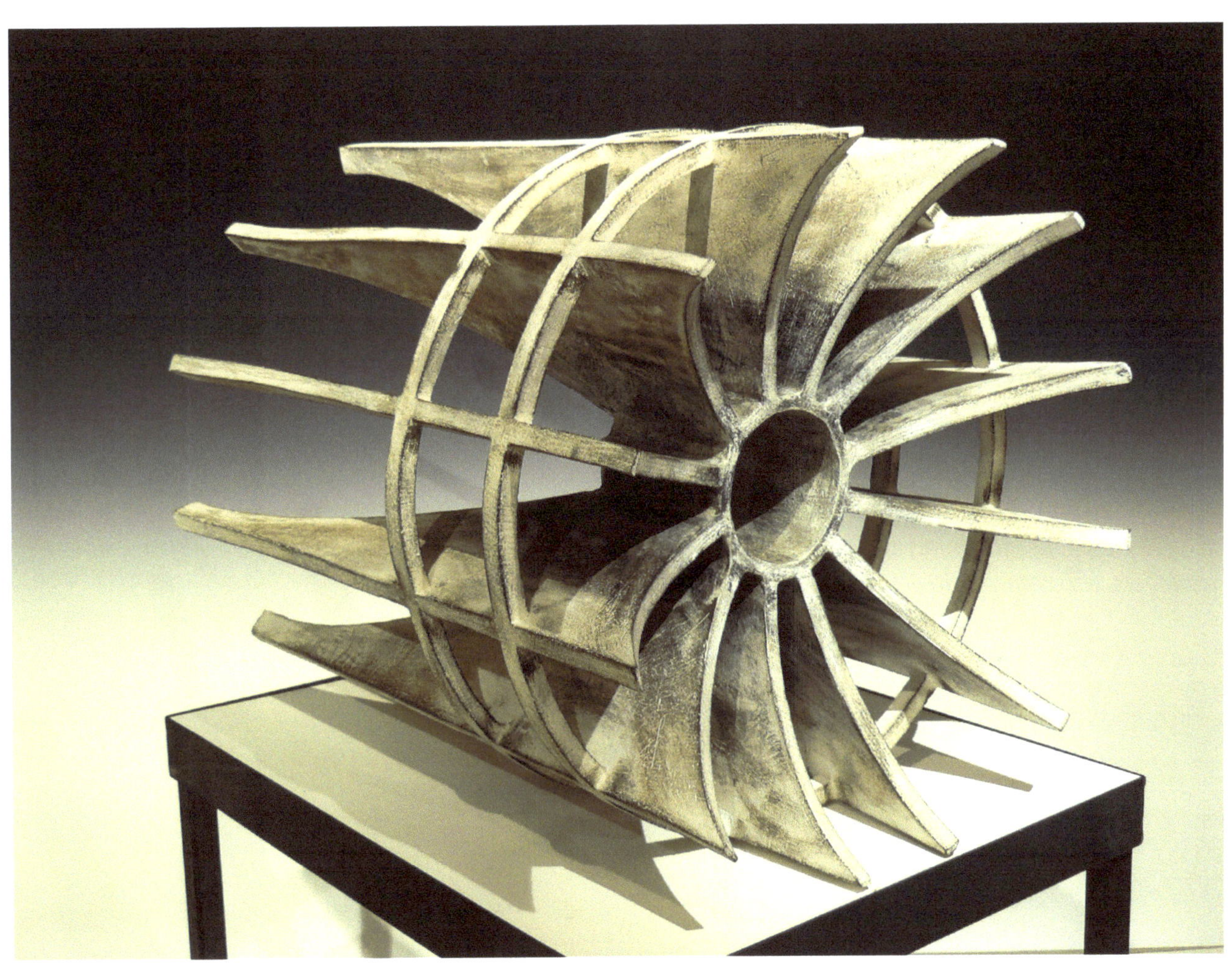

Peter Christian Johnson
Turbine #1: From the Construction Series, 2012
White earthenware, computer rendered
21 x 30 x 21 Inches

Handmade objects are a reflection of people and place long before the separation of utility from beauty. Nowhere is this more true than in the garments of indigenous cultures of Guatemala and Mexico. Huipils, blouses of Mayan women, relate their ancient and modern histories through the weave and design of every handmade piece of clothing. Not only do I admire Mayan huipils as symbols of identity and protectors of culture, I feel a deep connection with fellow craftswomen who spend hours stitching them by hand. After being surrounded by these textiles during the 2 years I lived in Guatemala I find them extraordinarily visually appealing, as well as having a deep connection to that place. As I come to understand my own diverse cultural and personal experiences I aim to combine these influences with my personality to secure a sense of self and belonging in a transcultural society.

I am beginning to define my larger goals and build a vision for how I can use my passion for pottery as a vehicle to unite people. I am a humanitarian at heart and have an intense desire to build understanding and compassion between diverse people and cultures. I see potential to do this through interacting with diverse people to inform my design, the layers of meaning I create, the use of my work itself, and how my work gets into communities to find users.

Lauren Karle is presently a graduate student at Kansas State University.

Lauren Karle | MANHATTAN KANSAS

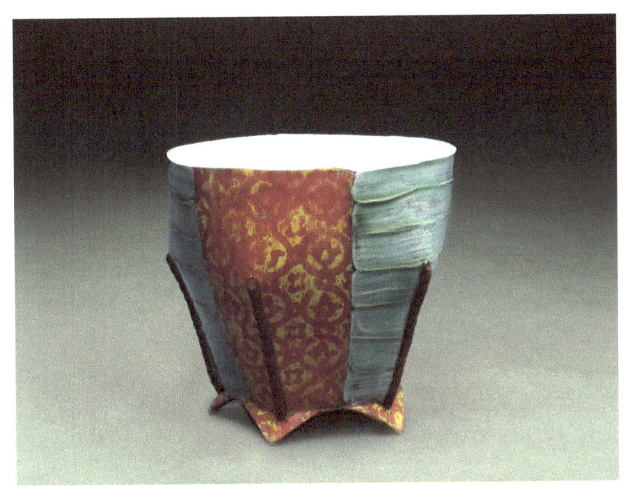

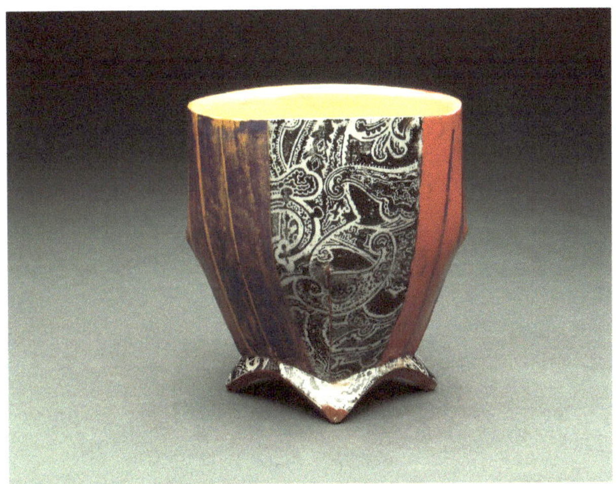

Lauren Karle
Cup, 2011
Earthenware, slip transfers
4 x 4 x 4 Inches

Lauren Karle
Cup, 2012
Earthenware, slip transfers
3.5 x 4 x 4 Inches

I am drawn to clay because of its endless possibilities for construction and surface finishes and am fascinated with the female form as it allows me to be personal but not self-indulgent, self-referential yet universal. I am inspired by a number of different artifacts; the antique "Santos" or religious figures of Central and South America, exquisitely rendered and deconstructed 19th and early 20th century porcelain doll heads from France and Germany, early American Folk Art, and African tribal sculpture.

The use of imagery from another time and place gives the work an ageless sensibility, but its exploration of personal narrative makes it solidly contemporary.

Margaret Keelan's work has been exhibited extensively across the United States: Seattle, Sun Valley, Chicago, St. Louis, New York, and notably, Tempe, AZ where she received a purchase award at the 2009 NCECA Biennial Exhibition. She has presented lectures on her work at Sheridan College, Ontario, CCACA Davis, SOFA New York and NCECA Baltimore. Her work has been showcased in *New Ceramics*, *Ceramics Art and Perception*, and *Ceramics Monthly*. Keelan is Associate Director and Ceramics Professor at the Academy of Art University in San Francisco.

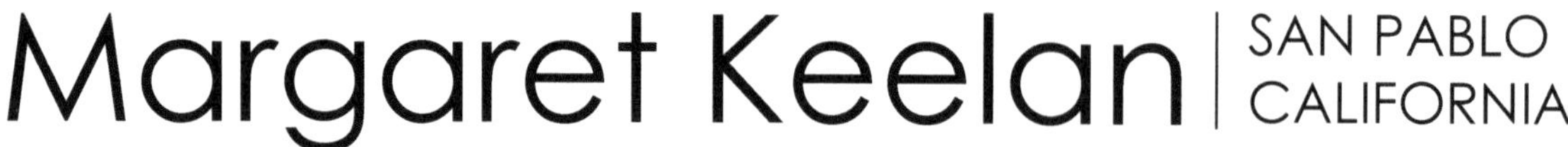

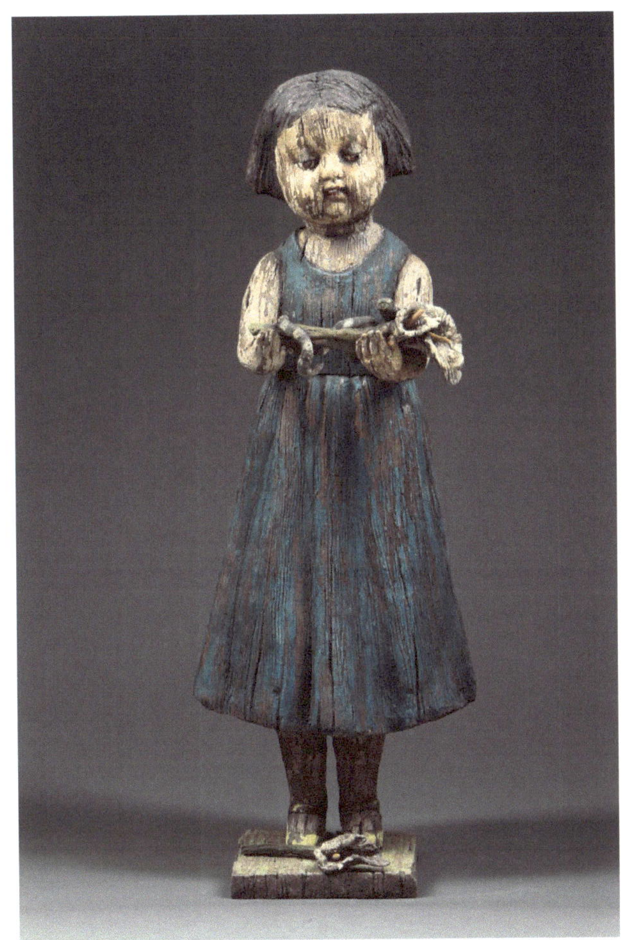

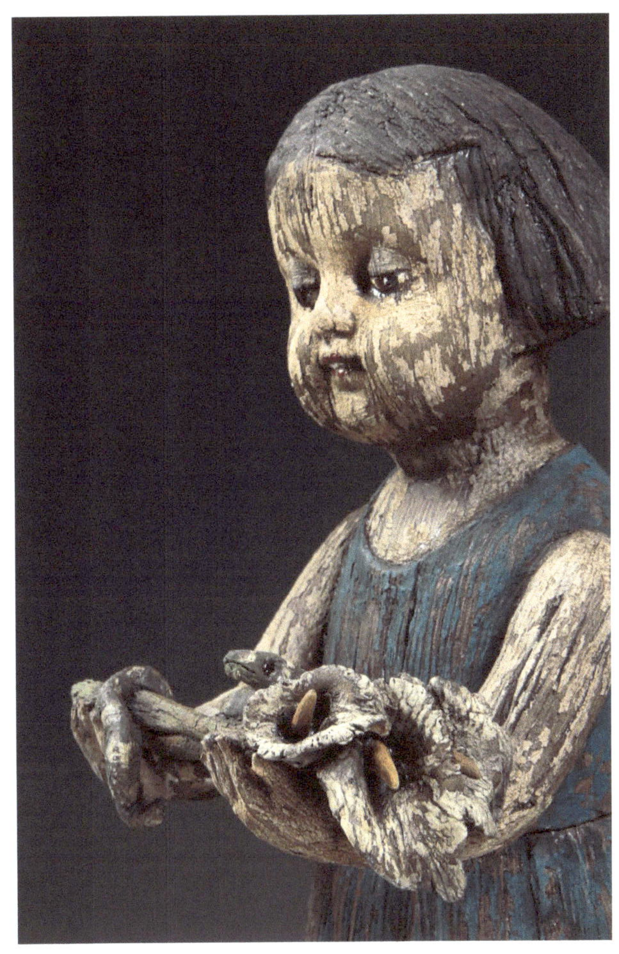

Margaret Keelan
Bouquet, 2011
Stoneware, stains, glaze
24 x 9 x 8 Inches
Photo Scott McCue

The domesticated canine specifically intrigues me because of its long-standing relationship with us and the technological world we create. Dogs exists in environments that are designed for our needs, not theirs. We continually strive to control and tame them to fit our desires. However, dogs too have adapted and learned to indulge in the comfort we created for ourselves. These are now the established environments of dogs, previously associated with wildness. They became dependent upon us, demonstrating both acceptance and opportunistic impulses. In our effort to seek power and control, various cultures have a disposable attitude of detachment toward dogs. Dogs are commodities used for work, protection, transportation, companionship, even food. In the domestication process, this animal species evolved to be accustomed to serve us.

In this work, I have represented one of the Chinese guardian lion pairs, known as Shishi or Foo Dogs. The lion (cat) is interacting with a naturalistic dog. As pairs, the lions traditionally stood in front of Chinese imperial palaces and were believed to have protective mythic powers. The lions are always created in pairs, male and female, as a symbol of strength. The naturalistic dog, however, acts as a replacement to the second lion and disrupts the harmony that otherwise would have existed.

Marina Kuchinski earned a BFA from the Bezalel Academy of Art and Design in Jerusalem and an MFA from Pennsylvania State University. She has been a visiting artist. Additionally, Kuchinski has received grants, awards and has particpated in juried exhibitions. Kuchinski has been exhibiting extensively nationally and internationally, including the Archie Bray Foundation, San Diego Art Institute, NCECA Conference and numerous university galleries. Kuchinski has taught at a number of colleges and since 2000, she has been a professor of art, teaching ceramics and drawing at the College of DuPage in IL. She is represented by the Obsidian Gallery in Tucson AZ.

Marina Kuchinski | WHEATON ILLINOIS

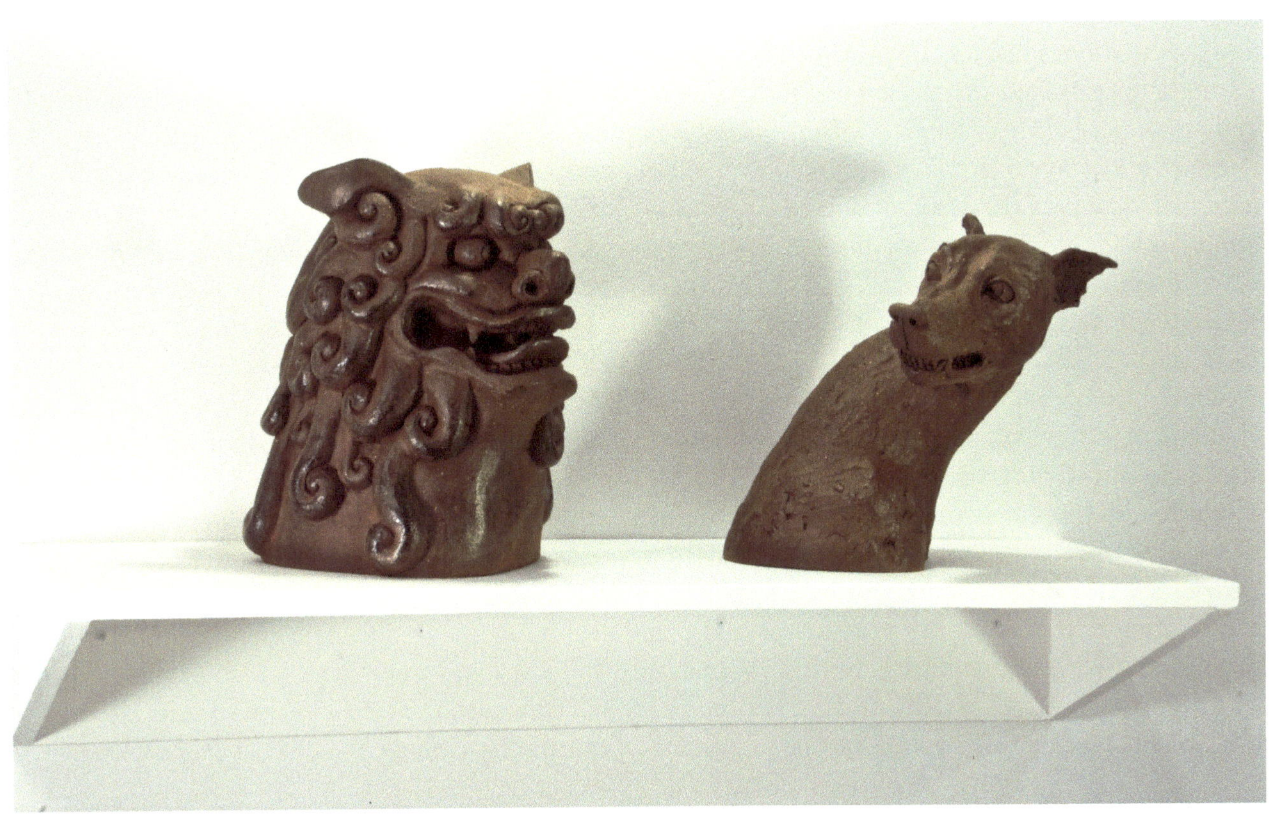

Marina Kuchinski
First World Problems, 2012
Earthenware
12 x 27 x 10 Inches

Skeletons are a recurring theme in my work. My fascination with skeletons and skulls is primarily from exposure to Mexican culture and immersion in the underground music scene. I do not see skeletons as representations of death. The Mexican folk artist Alfonso Castillo has influenced my approach to ceramics, in imagery, construction methods and surface decoration. Much of his work epitomizes the celebration of the Day of the Dead. This holiday is marked to recall persons that have passed and as a reminder of our own mortality. Relating this to Ecumene, specifically the concept of the permanently inhabited portion of the earth, in certain circumstances finding fragments of bones is the only evidence of human habitation. Skeletons are the foundation of our flesh and after decay the only thing that remains. Nearly every culture on earth uses skulls to convey a warning. In modern American pop culture, skeletons can say "I'm a badass stay away" or "I'm cool." Either way skulls are here to stay.

Originally from Fort Knox, Kentucky, Max Lehman (Max L) presently resides in Nambe, New Mexico where he maintains his studio and is rehabilitating an old family farm with his partner and four dogs. Lehman attended college at Arizona State University in the early 80's, studying for a degree in intermedia (now known as media arts), while also studying Pre-Columbian art history. Most of his training in ceramics came by practical experience. He apprenticed at the F&R Pottery Studio in Cave Creek, north of Phoenix, during his college years. He later went on to work for the Red Horse Clay Company, managing the production studio and designing images for their line of southwestern interior accessories. Currently Lehman is both a full-time artist and webmaster which provides the unique perspective of daily moving between a virtual sphere to the tactile realm of clay. He occasionally teaches both disciplines at the Santa Fe Community College.

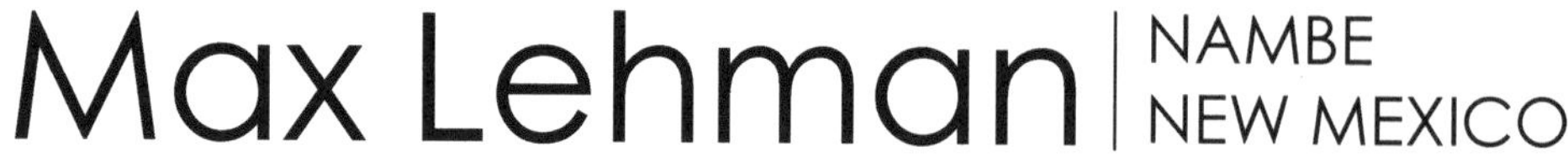

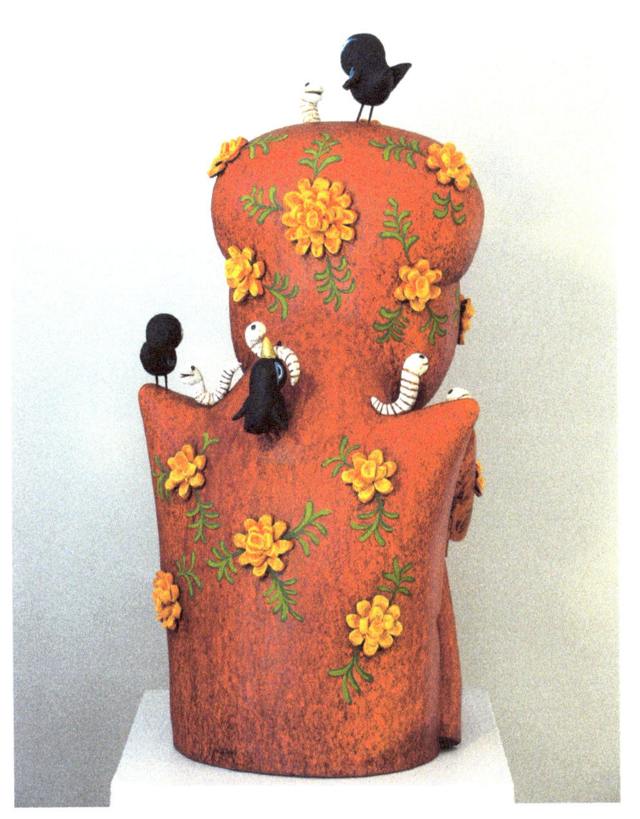

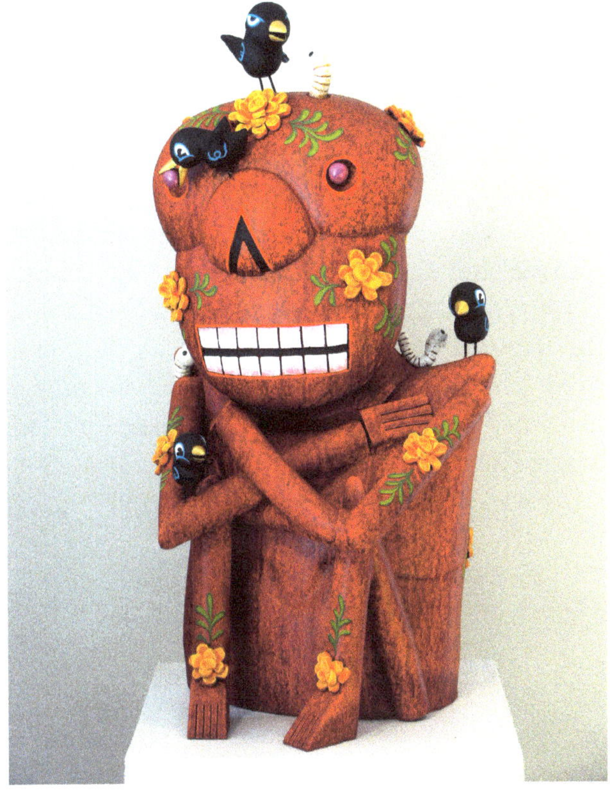

Max Lehman
Red Skeleton and Black Crows, 2011
Earthenware, underglaze, paint
27 x 18 x 15 Inches

The work is a bridge between the ancient ethic of the aesthetic experience as the primacy of the visual arts and a contemporary studio ethic, or practice. Its roots in Asia, Islamic art, and England allude to structure, form, history, and technology both past and present. What is ancient is renewed, not merely repeated, but refreshed, abstracted, and alive, always unfolding in a dialogue between beauty and the unknown.

Andrew Martin earned his BFA from the Kansas City Art Institute and his MFA from Alfred University. He has had two residencies at the Archie Bray Foundation, been a resident in the Arts-Industry Program at the Kohler Company, and has been awarded two Artist Fellowship Grants from the National Endowment for the Arts. He has taught over ninety workshops in the United States, Canada, and Europe, exhibited nationally and internationally, written essays and articles for *American Ceramics* and *Ceramics Monthly*, and been a moderator and demonstrator at the annual conference of the National Council on Education for the Ceramic Arts (NCECA). His book, "The Essential Guide to Mold Making and Slip Casting" has become the standard text on the subject. The revised and expanded edition of this book, published by Lark Books, was released in March 2007. Martin lives in Maria Hoop, The Netherlands.

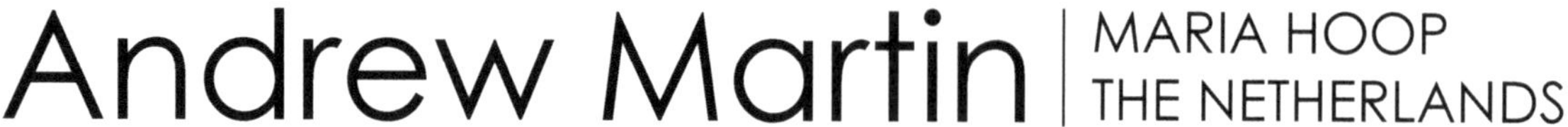

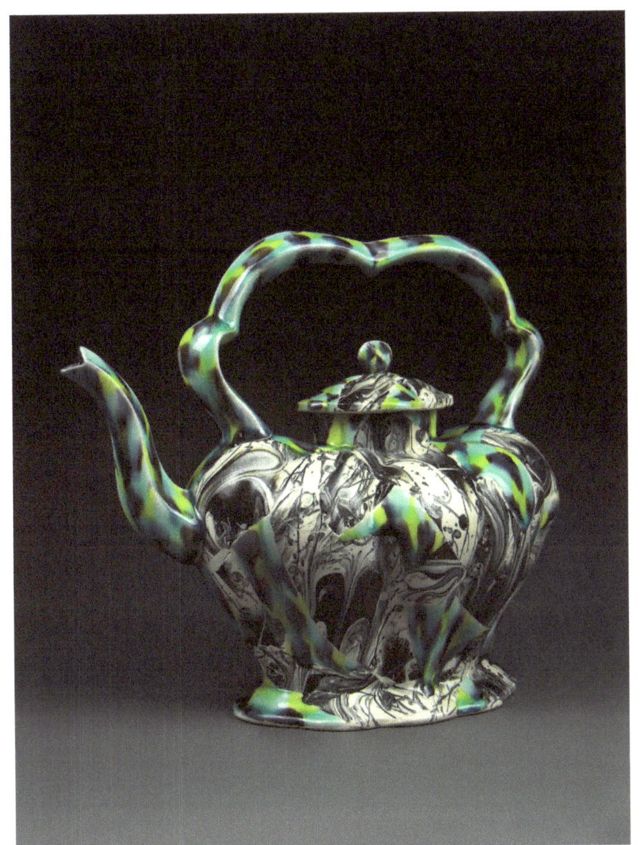

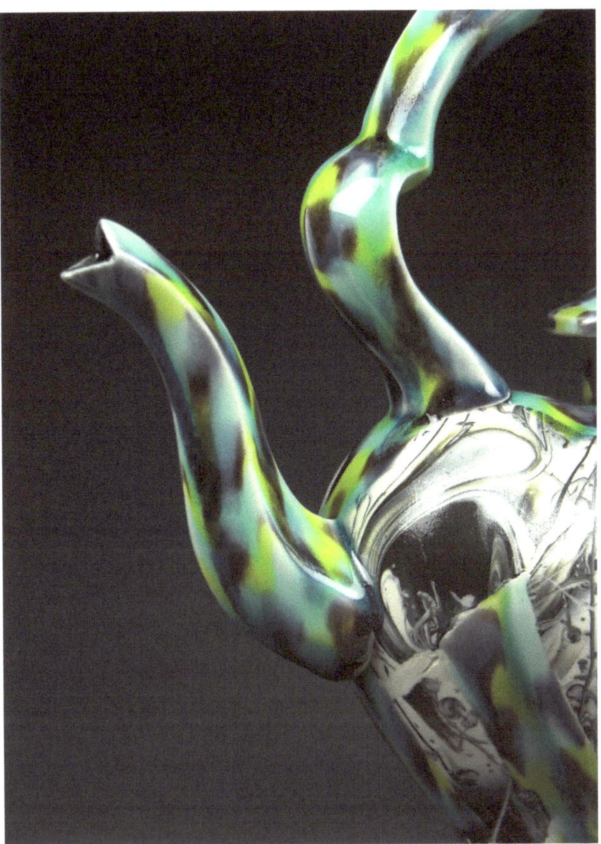

Andrew Martin
Kimono, 2012
Marbleized porcelain, polychrome glazes
11.5 x 13 x 6.5 Inches

My works address notions of the emotional human psychology, one that perhaps creates a singular moment of empathy for an object we all know and is part of the universal human experience. Furniture possesses an undeniable relationship to the body. Through our use of objects like a bureau or bed, they become extensions and tools that fit our bodies. We've all had the experience of sitting in a chair that is shorter than we expected; the point is that a bodily expectation exists, one created through repetition and routine. It is embedded in the volume, weight and height of an object. It is embedded in our bodies. As a result of this proportional nature of furniture, I am exploring the chair as a metaphor for the emotional human body.

Lauren Mayer is a ceramic artist who lives and works in Colorado. She received her BFA from Michigan State University and her MFA from the University of Colorado, Boulder. Currently, she teaches at Metropolitan State College of Denver.

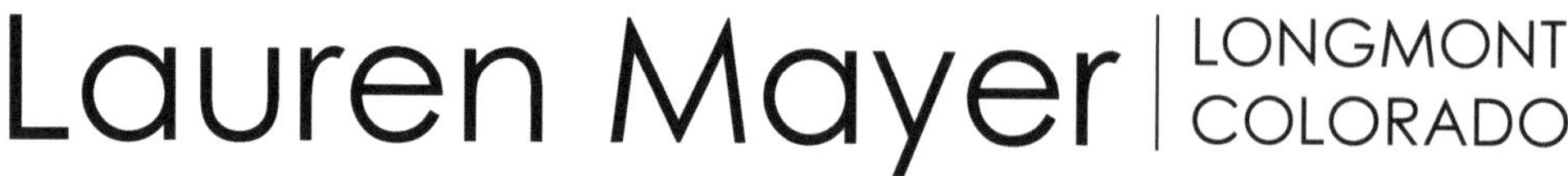

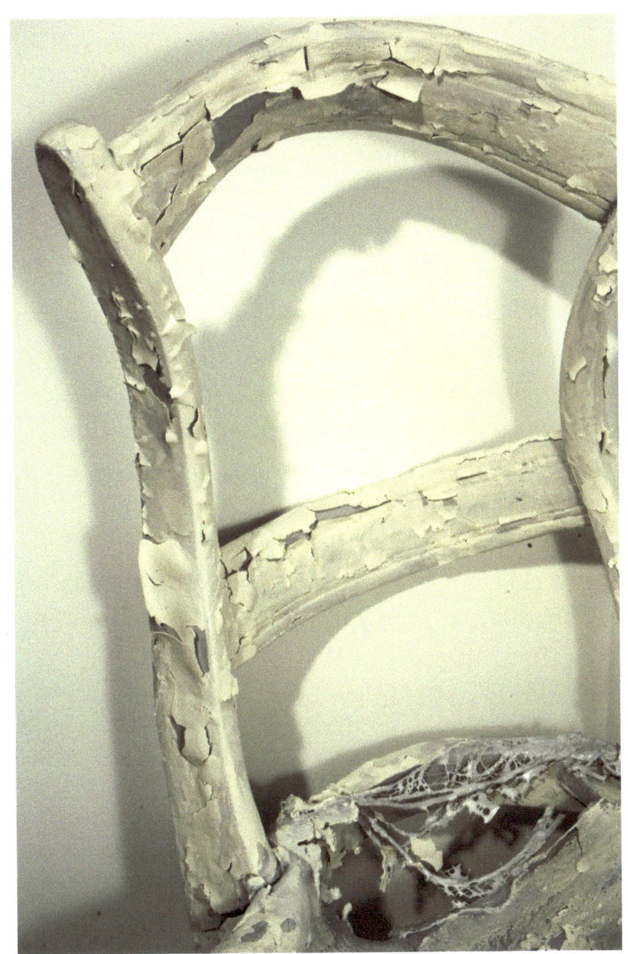

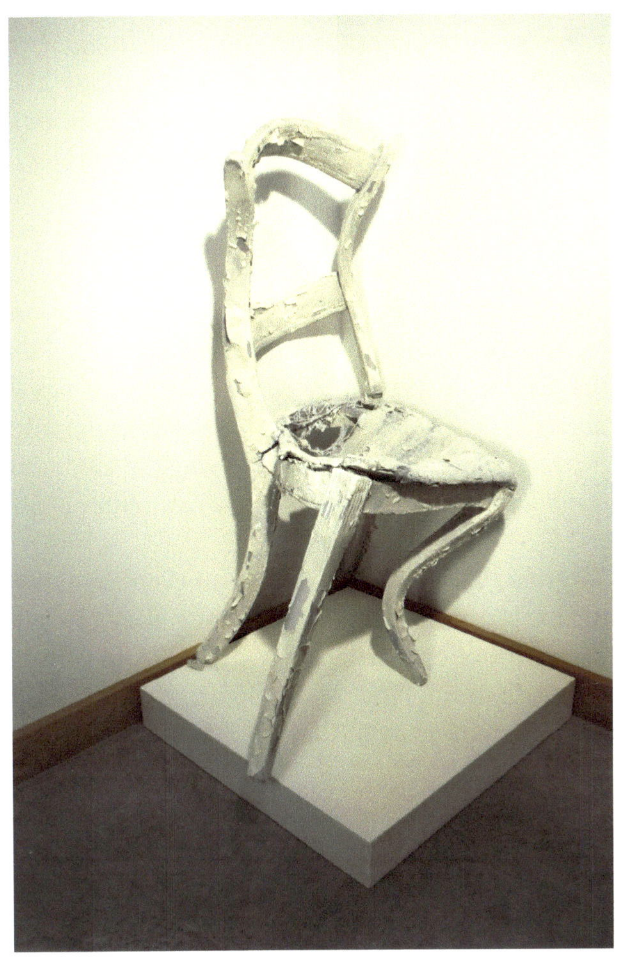

Lauren Mayer
Untitled, 2011
Cast porcelain
34 x 20 x 20 Inches

From Mississippi mud to English bone china, Mexican sand and Arizona gold, I travel throughout the world collecting materials to bring back to my studio. Found materials (clays, rocks, dirt) generate form and express the cyclical nature of ceramics. Stone decays into clay, is formed and then fired, simulating the conditions of geologic metamorphosis through magma-like temperatures that vitrify the material back into stone.

These clay forms are cylindrical controls, easily influenced by the variable, the contamination of dirt and debris. The process of wheel-throwing, the creation of a pure cylinder, is a repeatable process which allows me to experiment with variations of material. I throw with loose, gestural moves, stretching and pushing the pots to the limits of stability, while inclusions displace the clay, creating unexpected shifts of balance and texture. The pots are quickly cut from the wheel and dropped onto raised rings or boxes. The clay is free to move as it begins the drying process, allowing the materials within the clay body to shift and coagulate, refining the pot's shape and center of gravity.

Virginia Pates digs and invents an ever-changing palette of clays for her thin and gesturally-thrown forms. Her underlying deftness as a glaze chemist shows through in her unusual range of glaze colors and atmospheric surfaces. With a MFA in Ceramics from the University of Wales, she has taught ceramics in England, Mississippi and Arizona. Pates is currently Artist in Residence at the historic artists' community of Rancho Linda Vista in Oracle, Arizona.

Virginia Pates | ORACLE ARIZONA

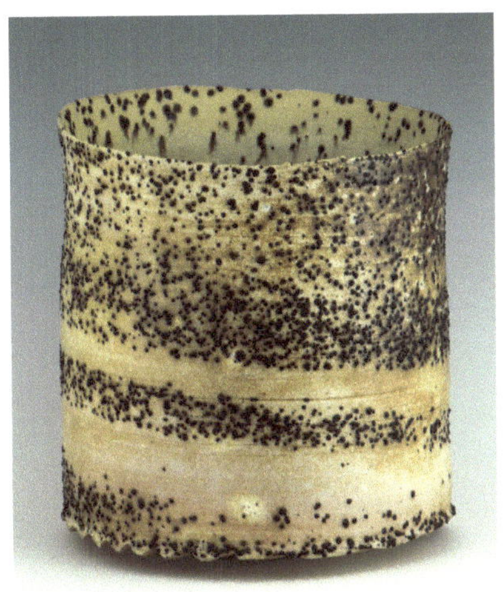

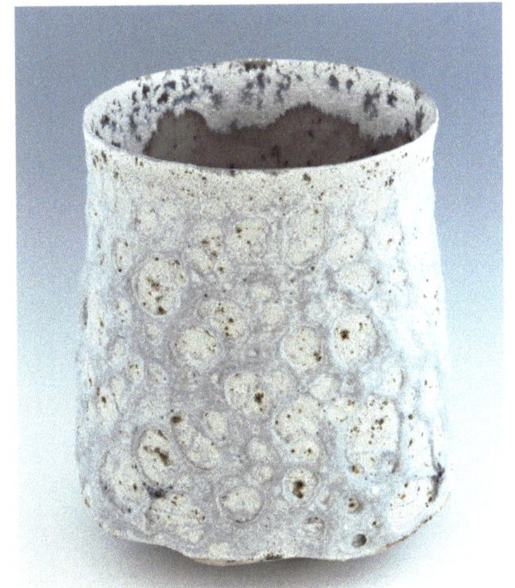

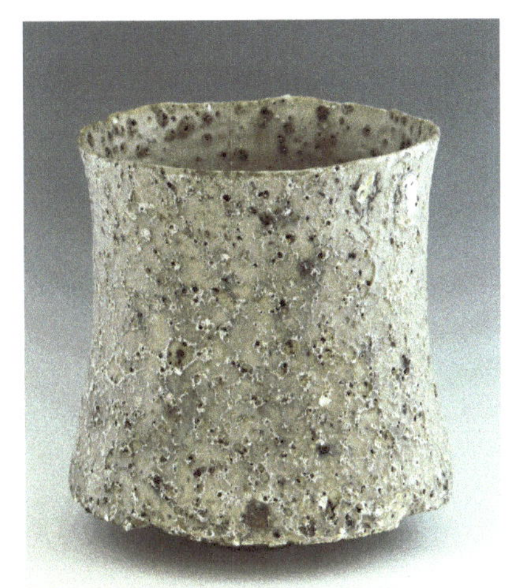

Virginia Pates
Playa Negra in Soda, 2011
Porcelain, black sand, glaze
7 x 6.5 x 6.5 Inches

Virginia Pates
Clarkdale Brick, 2011
Porcelain, natural brick clay, glaze
8 x 7 x 7 Inches

Virginia Pates
Verde Dirt, 2011
White stoneware, gravel, flashing slip, glaze
7 x 7.5 x 7.5 Inches

Global Interface. As a ceramic artist, my work has been influenced both by the rich environment of ceramic sculptors I have been surrounded by in California, but also the larger context of humanist sculpture throughout the world, especially the figurative art in Italy and Mexico.

The content of my current work is certainly a global issue. The urgency of addressing the health of life on our planet is of primary importance, and the solutions must be addressed globally. Artists have historically been the ones to bring to light the pressing issues of the world. I feel passionate about this role during my time here on this planet.

Lisa Reinertson completed her MFA at UC Davis in 1984, studying with Robert Arneson, and Manuel Neri. She has taught ceramics and figurative sculpture courses at several universities and colleges in Northern California including California State University, Chico, Santa Clara University and University of California, Berkeley. Her ceramic work has been in exhibitions and museums nationally and internationally including the Crocker Art Museum, the Oakland Museum, Arizona State University Art Museum and Museo Internationale Della Ceramica, Faenza, Italy. Reinertson has completed over 20 public commissions. Reinerston currently works from her studio in Benicia and teaches at the San Francisco Art Institute.

Lisa Reinertson | BENICIA CALIFORNIA

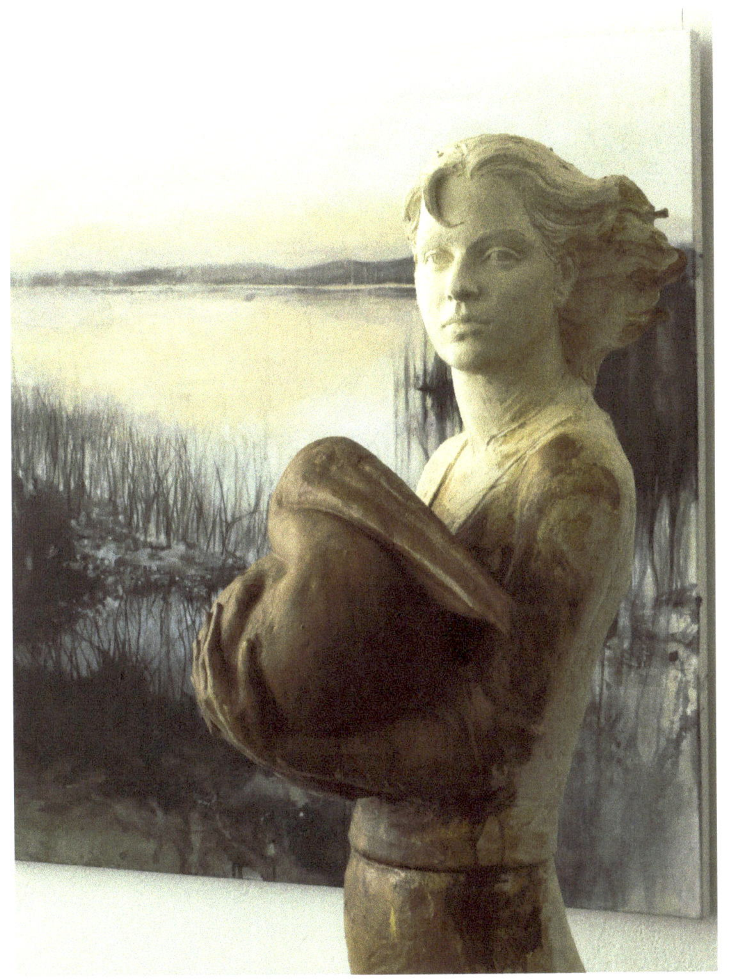

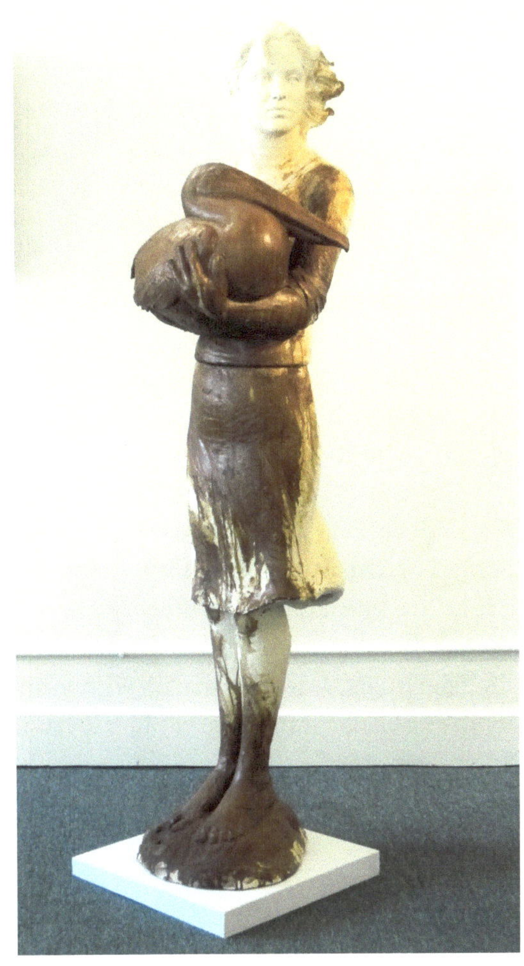

Lisa Reinertson
Neptune's Daughter, 2011
Ceramic
72 x 18 x 15 Inches

In my work I consider the animals in our world. Whether pets or in the wild, humanity has used animals as expressive symbols since the first representations created on cave walls. The exhibition's title, Global Interface calls to my mind the respect that we all must have for the various beings on this Earth, a planet which has grown so much smaller through advances in technology and communication. As much as the premise for this exhibition represents a joining of minds and exchange of ideas, it also asks us to consider common threads that have endured throughout history. Ceramics is an ancient tradition, the materials literally of the Earth, and while modern science has enhanced and added some amount of ease to production, the dynamic remains constant throughout time.

I feel as though I am working on a daily basis with forms and figures that are part of our collective unconscious: concentrating on the energy and interior of an animal hopefully brings the viewer a sense of safety and reminder of compassion - much needed in what has become an increasingly scary world.

Kari Reeves has worked in various media throughout her life, studying painting and glass at the School of The Museum of Fine Art in Boston, as well as the Skowhegan School of Painting and Sculpture in Maine. She reflects. "My training held me accountable for honesty of purpose and demanded that I possess a truly critical eye toward the quality of my work — both necessary for a lifetime in art. I deal primarily with animals and figures, secure in safe places, and am also intrigued by the concept of inanimate objects having feelings and an inner life."

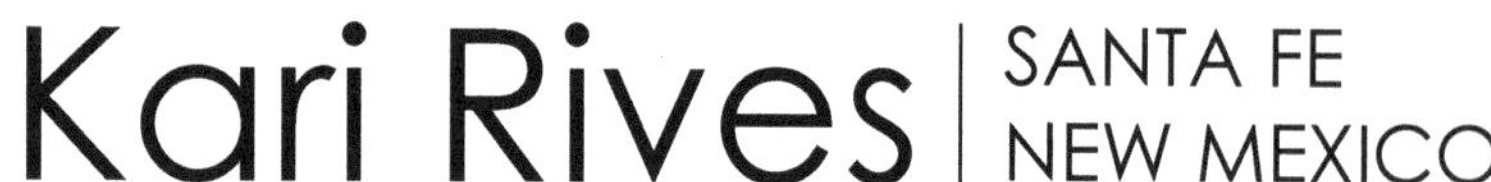

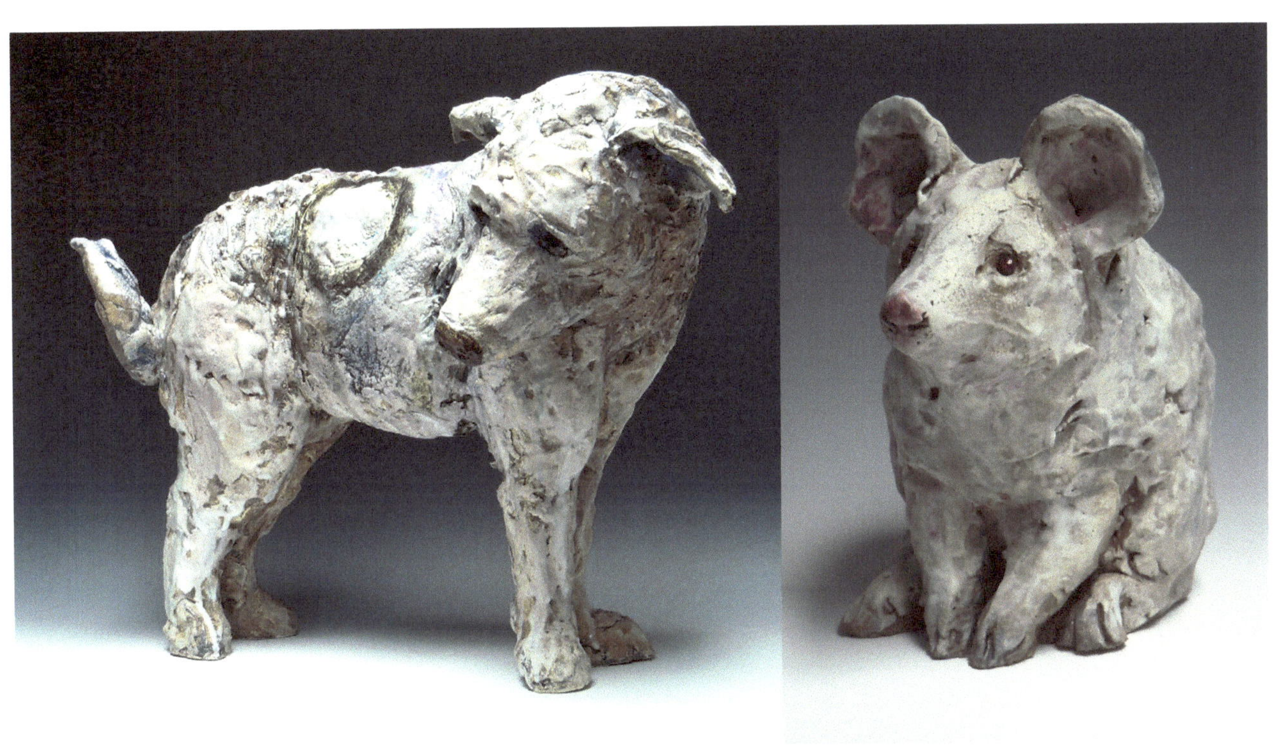

Kari Rives
Spot (Empty Nest), 2012
Clay, glazes with added pigments
16 x 23 x 10 Inches

Kari Rives
Lucy, 2012
Clay, glazes
7 x 5 x 7 Inches

"Punch" represents Anger as one of the Seven Deadly Sins. Metaphorically each punching bag in the cart (47—which was the age my brother was when he was murdered at his business) was made of porcelain clay......so if punched they break. Through this translation the act of anger is proven to be useless and serves no positive purpose but only ends in destruction. Each punching bag is silver which serves as a reflective surface allowing the viewer to see themselves in the piece. The shopping cart is used as a symbol of our consumer society and serves as a platform for each of the Seven Deadly Sins.

Virginia Scotchie is a ceramic artist and area head of ceramics at the University of South Carolina in Columbia, SC. She holds a BFA in Ceramics from University of North Carolina, Chapel Hill and in 1985 completed her MFA at Alfred University in NY. Scotchie exhibits her work extensively throughout the United States and abroad, and has received numerous awards including the Sydney Meyer Fund International Ceramics Premiere Award from the Shepparton Museum in Victoria, Australia.

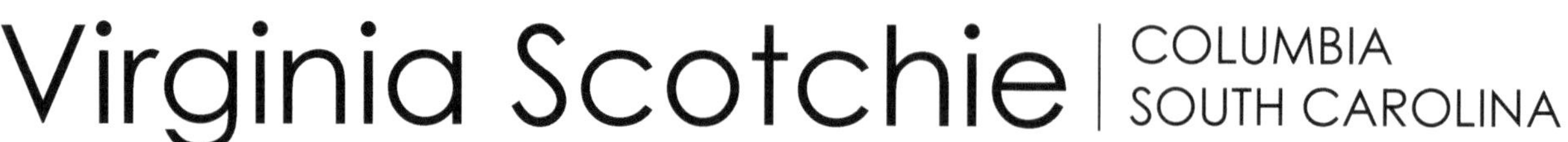

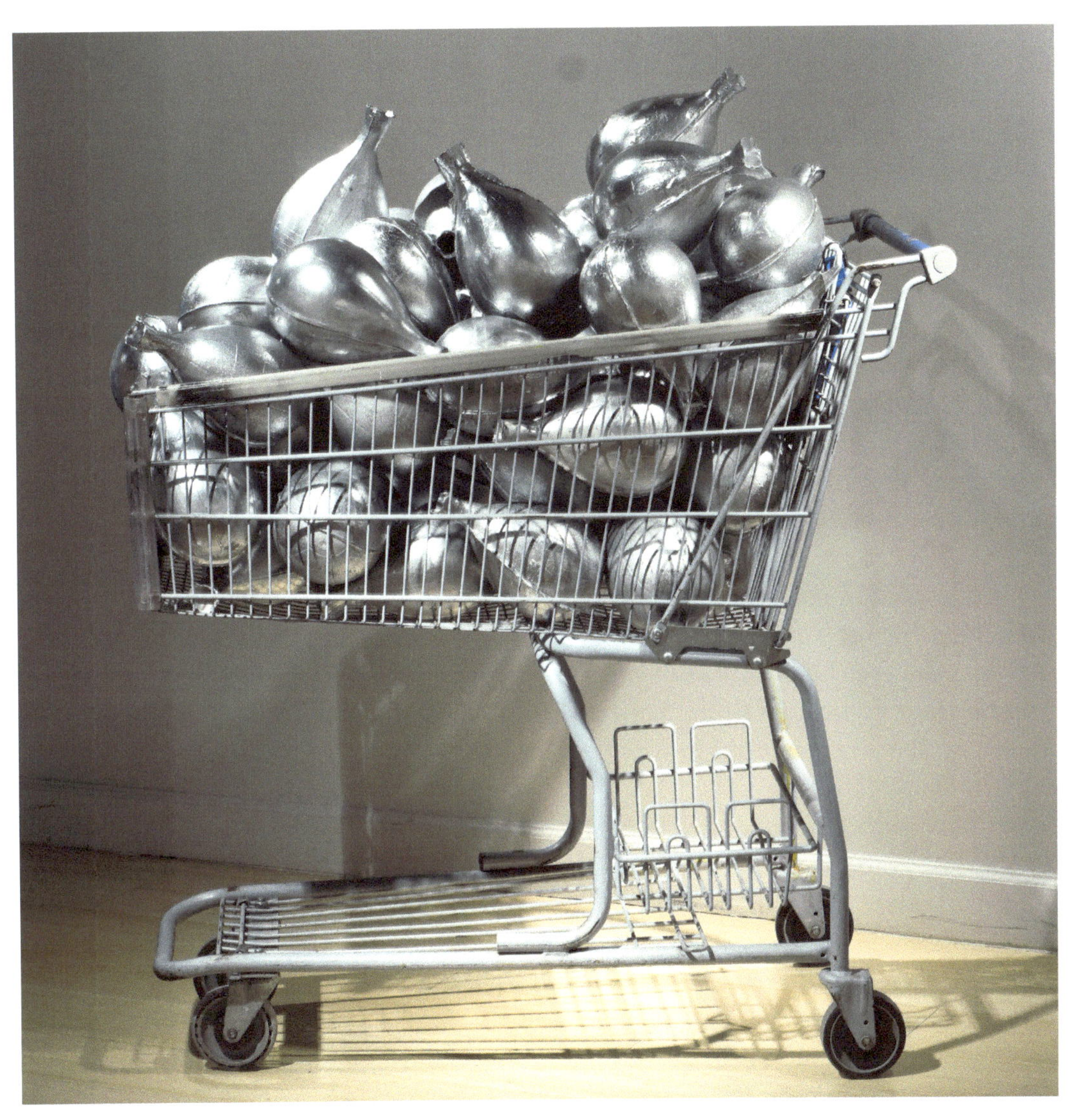

Virginia Scotchie
Seven Deadly Sins—Punch, 2012
Slip-cast porcelain, shopping cart
48 x 40 x 40 Inches
Photo by Gordon Humphries

People are the most compelling subjects for my art. Working with my hands in clay is my response to life today when we are constantly bombarded with so much information. I have to distance myself physically from this overload of stuff that I read, hear and see when I work. This includes depersonalizing the suffering and injustice that I know is always happening right now in the world.

Creating my work, on the other hand, is a very personal endeavor. Drawing and sculpting another person over an extended period of time is a very intimate thing to do, especially when they are naked. Many of the young men who have modeled for me lately strike me as being quite cautious as they find their way in the complicated times we live in. I think that when my drawing or sculpture succeeds it contains qualities of my model and myself that are very human. The empathy I feel towards people from all walks of life comes through. I aim to be a positive force for compassion and beauty which I believe go hand in hand.

The excellent eye/hand coordination I was born with has played a large role in my life as an artist. I knew as a child who loved playing ball sports that as I grew older, if I were lucky, my interest in making art would dominate my life. I am grateful to have been given the opportunity, ability and the desire to pursue that work which is the most meaningful to me. My sculpture combines all of the skills that I have accrued over years working in ceramics with my ever-growing empathy with my fellow human beings.

Suzanne Storer has only begun seeking national recognition for her figurative work this spring of 2012. So far she has exhibited at these national competitions: the 19th San Angelo National Ceramic Competition, Workhouse Arts Center Annual National 2012 and NCECA's Ecumene Exhibition. Storer's ceramic vessels, platters and sculptures are in public and private collections throughout the USA including the St. George Art Museum in Utah and the collection of John Frohnmayer, past Director of the National Endowment for the Arts. Through Art Access/VSA Utah, she has worked in clay with special needs children. Currently she is the monitor of the weekly community figure drawing sessions at Weber State University. Storer was a founding member of Clay Arts, Utah.

Suzzane Storer | OGDEN UTAH

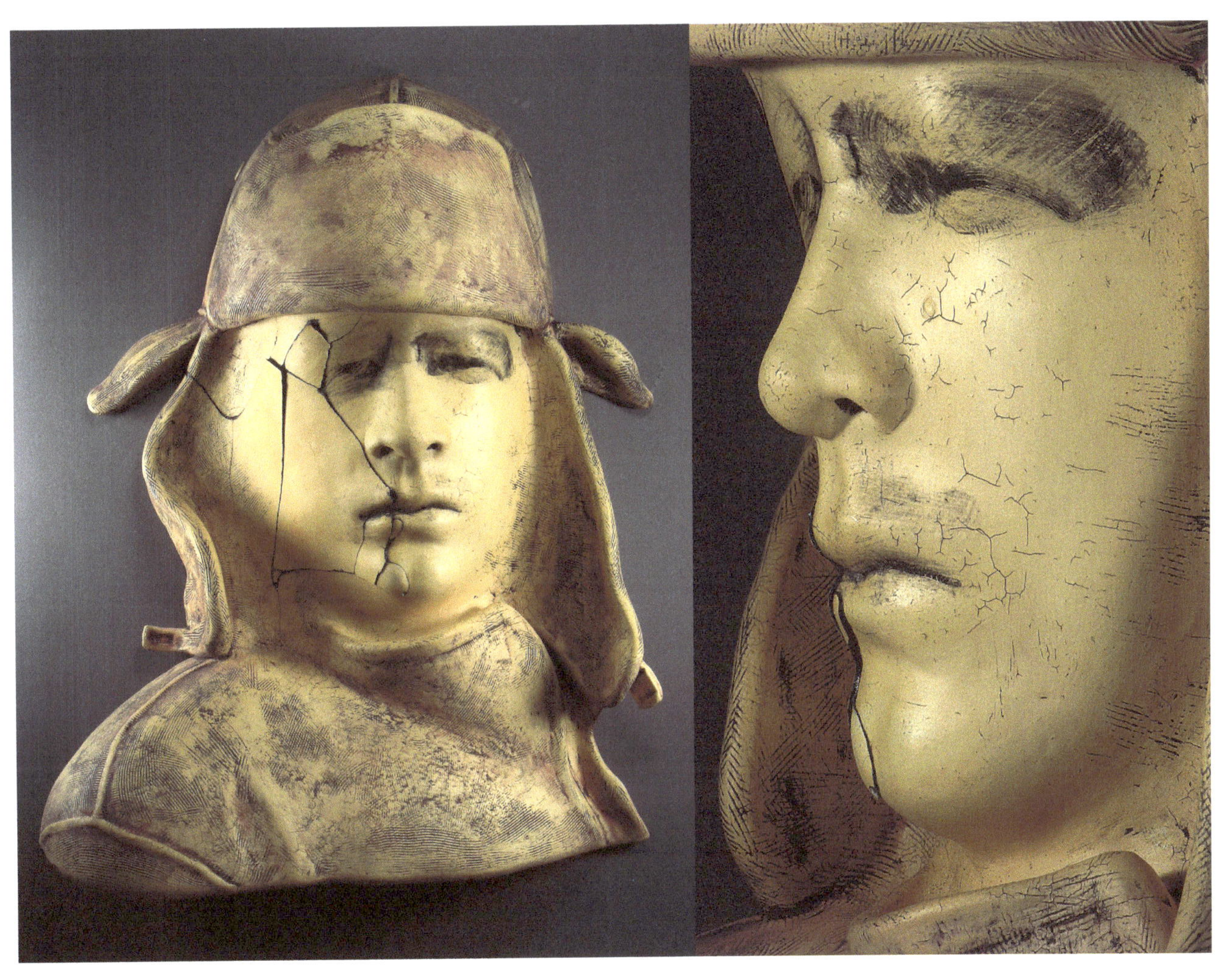

Suzzane Storer
Alec, My Son, 2012
Stoneware, terra sigillata, ceramics colorants, mixed media
21 x 16 x 7 Inches

This work, from a series called "Organic Banana", is about the effects of globalism. These bananas are you and I, simple persons living in the complicated world, while trying to be a little particular, trying to look at the better side of things... trying to be organic, by choosing pre-packaged processed foods instead of just fruits, veggies, fish and meat. These foods came from all over the world, so we can eat seasonal foods which are grown in the different parts of the world all year long. It is also talking about not just material, but the whole economical and environmental systems are affecting other parts of the world.

The Tsunami in Japan caused a serious environmental damage by the Nuclear Plant that was made by GE in the US. The whole bad economy started from US in 2008 is still affecting all over the world.

If we go to buy something, whether it is a car, food, clothes or toy, it is very difficult to find something was made in the US with just only US ingredients or parts.

That's how my works relate to the concept of Ecumene: Global Interface

Hirotsune Tashima earned his MFA from Alfred University, NY and BFA from Osaka University of Art. He received numerous grants including Pollock-Krasner Foundation, Arizona Commission on the Arts, Rotary International and Japanese Government. Hirotsune held more than 20 solo exhibitions in NY, Tokyo and Tucson Museum of Art, AZ. Private and Public Collection(s) includes, Auckland Museum, New Zealand;, Everson Museum of Art, NY; Jingdezhen Museum of Ceramics, China; The Banff Centre for the Arts, Canada, and that of the singer, David Bowie.

Hirotsune Tashima | TUCSON ARIZONA

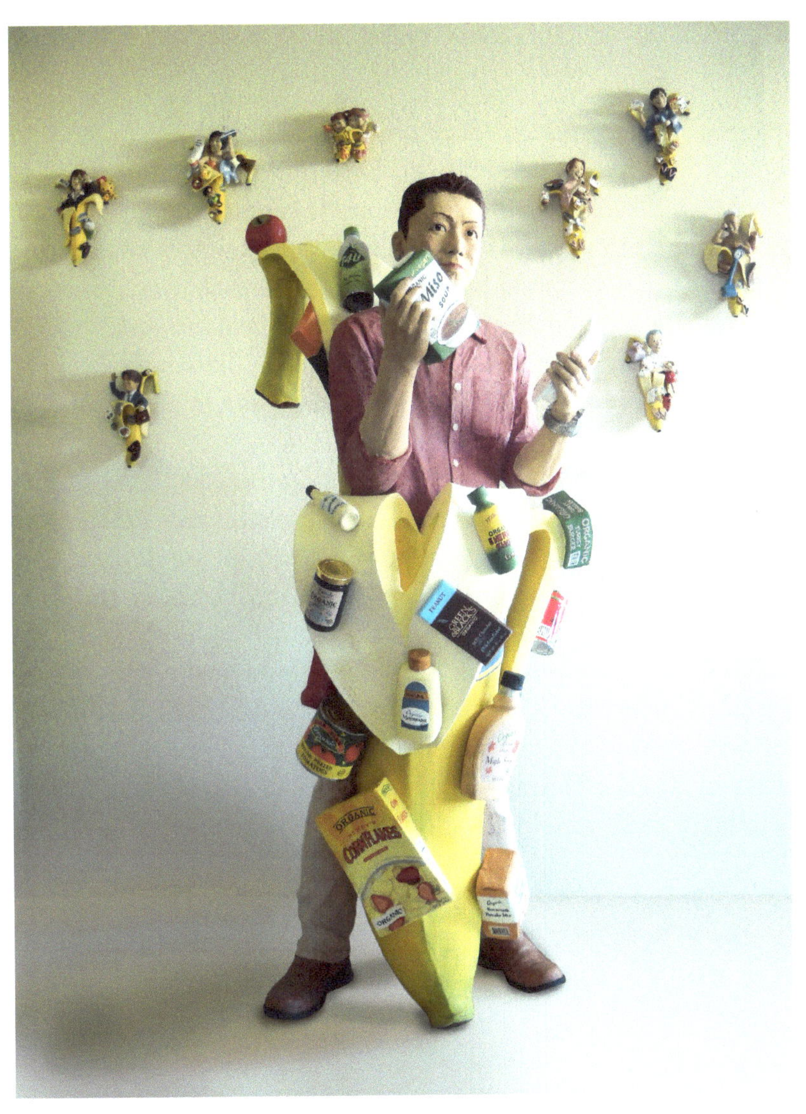

Hirotsune Tashima
Organic Banana in a Supermarket, 2011
Clay, glaze, lusters
67 x 30 x 28 Inches

Education, artist residencies, and exhibitions have brought me to a number of places across my own country as well as China, Taiwan, Italy, and Norway. Each time I arrived in a new place I began to look for relationships between the local environment and the ceramic work being produced there. Our physical environments have profound effects on the marks we choose to make in clay. It's no surprise then that every culture has developed a unique aesthetic that relates to the appearance of their specific locations. However the aesthetic differences are more than just the relationship of the local landscape to the colors, patterns, and shapes that compose an art object. An artist's choices of technique, craftsmanship, content, and resolution have a dramatic relationship to the history of that maker's culture.

It is important to me that the sculptures that I make should have a visual and social relationship to the place where I live. I also believe that the techniques that I use should recall the journey that I have taken as an American ceramist. My colored porcelain nerikomi techniques are influenced from my experiences in Taiwan, and my choices of specific colors and shapes come from my local Texas environment.

Katherine Taylor is a full time artist working in Little Elm,Texas, just north of Dallas. She earned her BFA from Texas A&M University – Commerce in 1998 and her MFA from Syracuse University in 2002. She was a resident artist at Skowhegan School of Painting and Sculpture in Maine in 2002, Snake Kiln Culture Park in Shui-Li, Taiwan in 2006, and Liv i Leire in Oslo, Norway in 2009. Her work has been exhibited nationally and internationally and is included in several museum collections.

Katherine Taylor | TUCSON ARIZONA

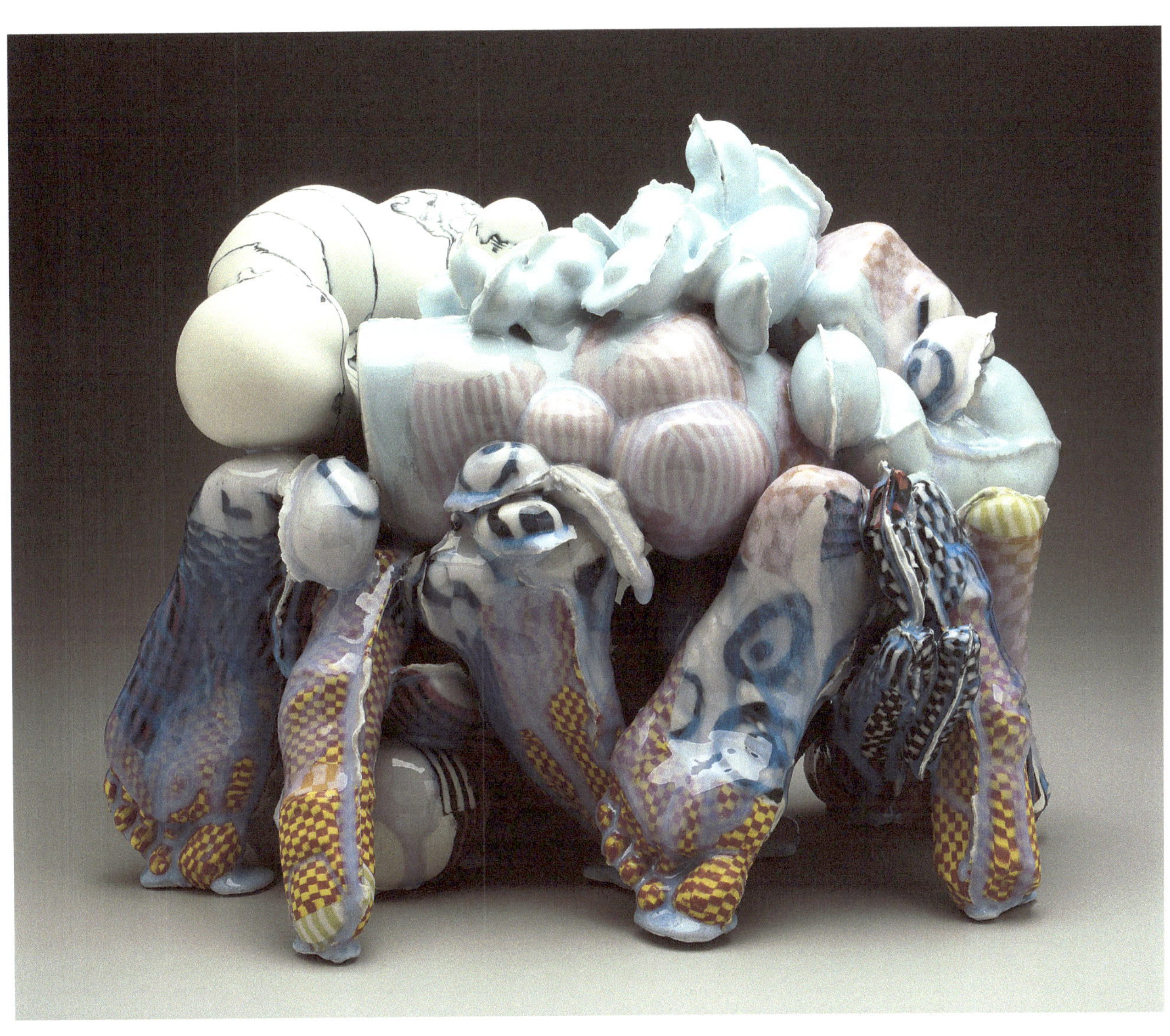

Katherine Taylor
One Cotton Bale, Texas Panhandle, 2011
Colored porcelain, glaze
15 x 18.5 x 30 Inches
Photo Harrison Evans

My ceramic sculptures reflect upon a variety of issues with a thoughtful, yet humorous and ironic tone. I am inspired by the potential of common everyday objects. I reproduce these objects primarily through slip-casting, and illustrate the surfaces with a variety of handpainted and screenprinted imagery. My narratives explore topics ranging from fairy tales, urban mythologies, consumer culture, societal expectations, etiquette, and coming of age issues. Stylistically, much of my imagery is pulled from somewhat "dated" sources that I find represent an idealized time in society and advertising. Such gems include instructional guides, cookbooks, old advertisements, and old family photos. Beneath the shiny veneer of these relics hides a complex and sometimes contradicting truth of what things seem to appear as upon first glance. In reflecting on my work relating to a larger global dialogue, my imagery stylistically reflects a distilled sugar coated "Americana" ideal, which brings into question ideas of consumerism, gender roles, what we value in society, and self-perception and worth in this modern age.

Shalene Valenzuela received a BA in Art Practice at the University of California, Berkeley and an MFA in Ceramics from California College of Arts and Crafts. She has participated in artist residencies at the Clay Studio of Missoula, the Archie Bray Foundation and Watershed Center for the Ceramic Arts. Valenzuela has been an instructor, guest artist and speaker at a number of art centers, colleges, and universities—her work has been featured in several group and solo exhibitions nationally. Her upcoming solo exhibition at the Missoula Art Museum will open in September 2012.

Shalene Valenzuela | MISSOULA MONTANA

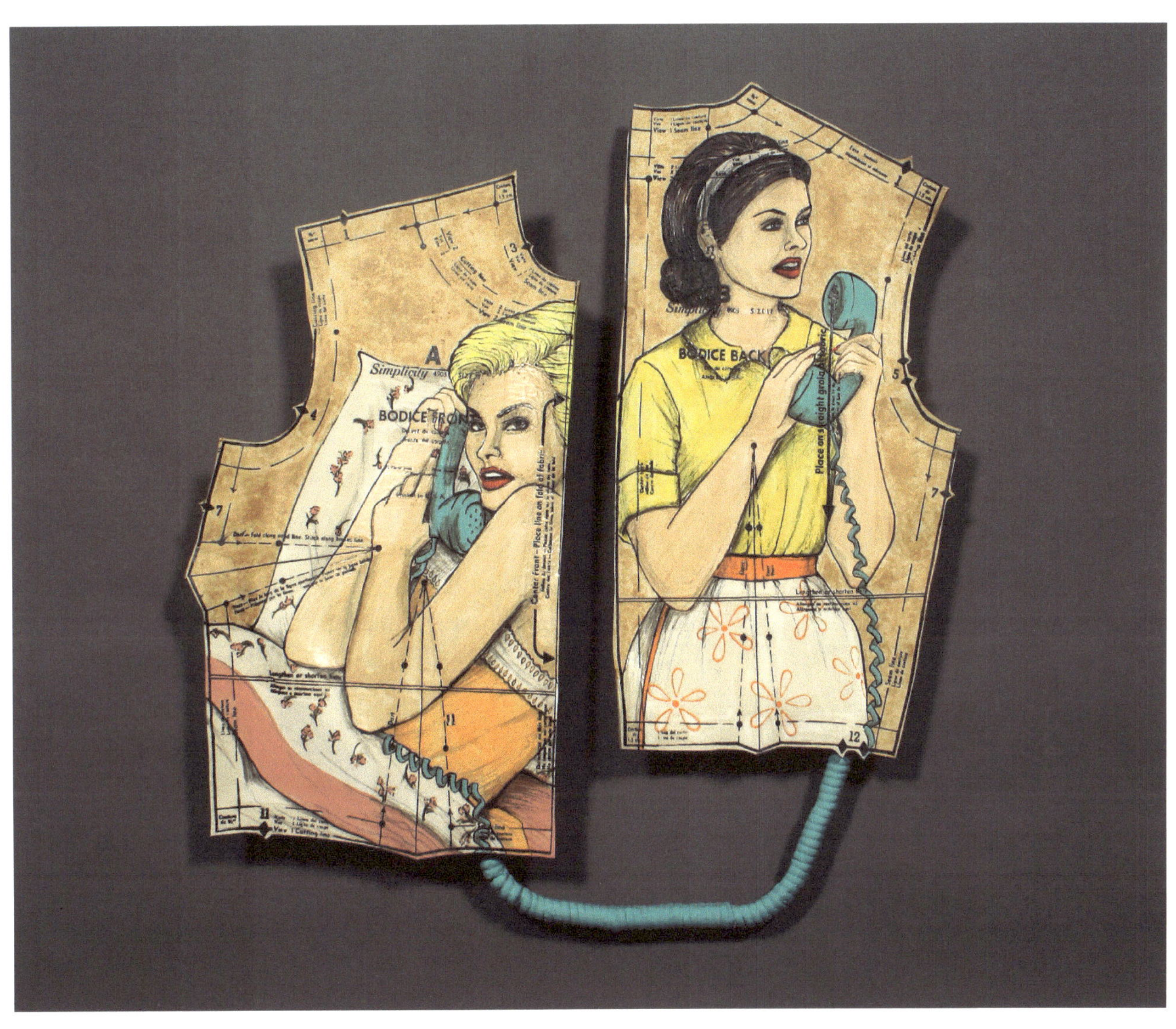

Shalene Valenzuela
Follow the Pattern: Let's Play Telephone, 2012
Porcelain, underglaze illustration print transfer
17 x 16 x 2 Inches

This body of work is inspired by the genre of still-life painting (functioning traditionally as a reminder of mortality) and particularly by the compositions of Chardin. Simplified but realistic representations of animals are contrasted with cartoonishly glazed and artificially bright and vibrant elements (dripping oranges, bright yellow canaries, flowing drips). The combination of both jarring and decorative elements correlates with the complexity and strain of our attempt to understand our mortality in its entirety. "Cameo" has roots in 18th century European painting, but represents a distinctly contemporary and American attitude towards its timeless subject matter.

Monica Van den Dool is a long-time lecturer in ceramics at San Jose State University (CA) as well as an adjunct instructor at various colleges/universities, including the University of California, Berkeley and the California College of the Arts. Her work has been exhibited at various national venues and is represented in the collections of the Arizona State University Ceramics Research Center, the Archie Bray Foundation, the DiRosa Preserve (CA) and Sandy Besser (NM). She has participated in artist residencies at the Archie Bray Foundation and Watershed Center for the Ceramic Arts, and in 2002 received an Emerging Artist award from NCECA. She earned a BA in English from Santa Clara University in 1990, her MFA from Montana State University in 1995 and now resides with her family in Oakland, CA.

Monica Van den Dool | OAKLAND CALIFORNIA

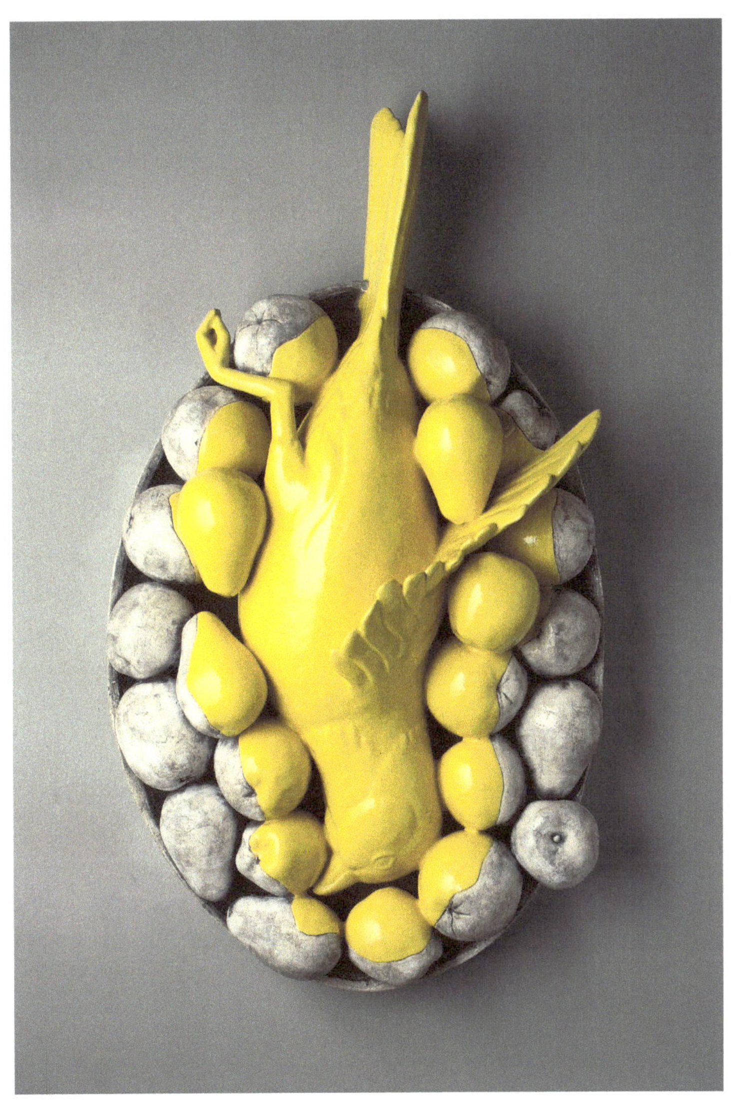

Monica Van den Dool
Cameo, 2011
Ceramic, slips, glazes 30 x 18 x 7 Inches

While the world's people and technology are hectically developing around us, there is an extremely important element that commonly goes unnoticed, Nature. It has an outstanding ability to regenerate out of the world's most basic materials. This concept can be recognized globally in even the most simple situations. My work is based on appreciation for the beauty that resides in growth. Sometimes, you have to go back to basics to find it.

In the beginning of creating this body of work, I had in mind these seed and egg shapes. I realized that they both had this incredible ability to become something much more intricate and beautiful, a living thing. My forms are stylized versions of objects found in nature. They do not usually directly represent actual seeds, but still have the potential to blossom into more intricate concepts.

When the individual objects are placed together, there is an immediate relationship between them. The relationship triggers a sense of animal or sometimes human quality. There is underlying emotion within each piece that doesn't require a specific language to understand. I decided to leave the surfaces bare to enforce their quiet pureness. There is nothing hidden and they are up for the interpretation of each individual viewer.

Katie White grew up on a farm in a small town with three siblings. As children, they used the outdoors to entertain ourselves. Having played in the dirt and clay in creeks her whole life, it wasn't until she went to Northern Illinois University that she took her first ceramics class. "I fell in love with it and switched my major from Photography to Ceramics." White recently graduated with a BFA in Ceramics and is determined to continue her career and actively become part of the ceramic world.

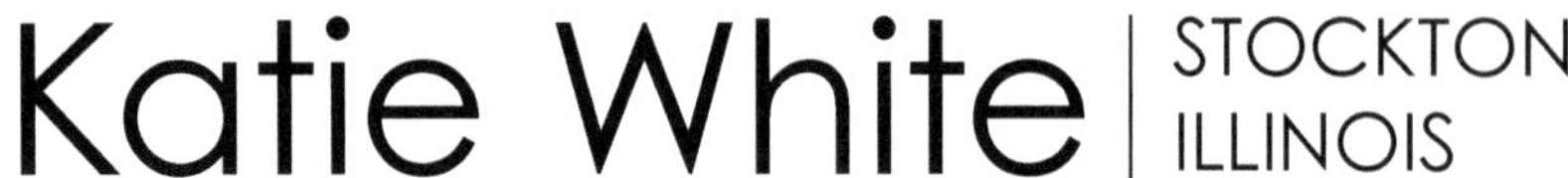

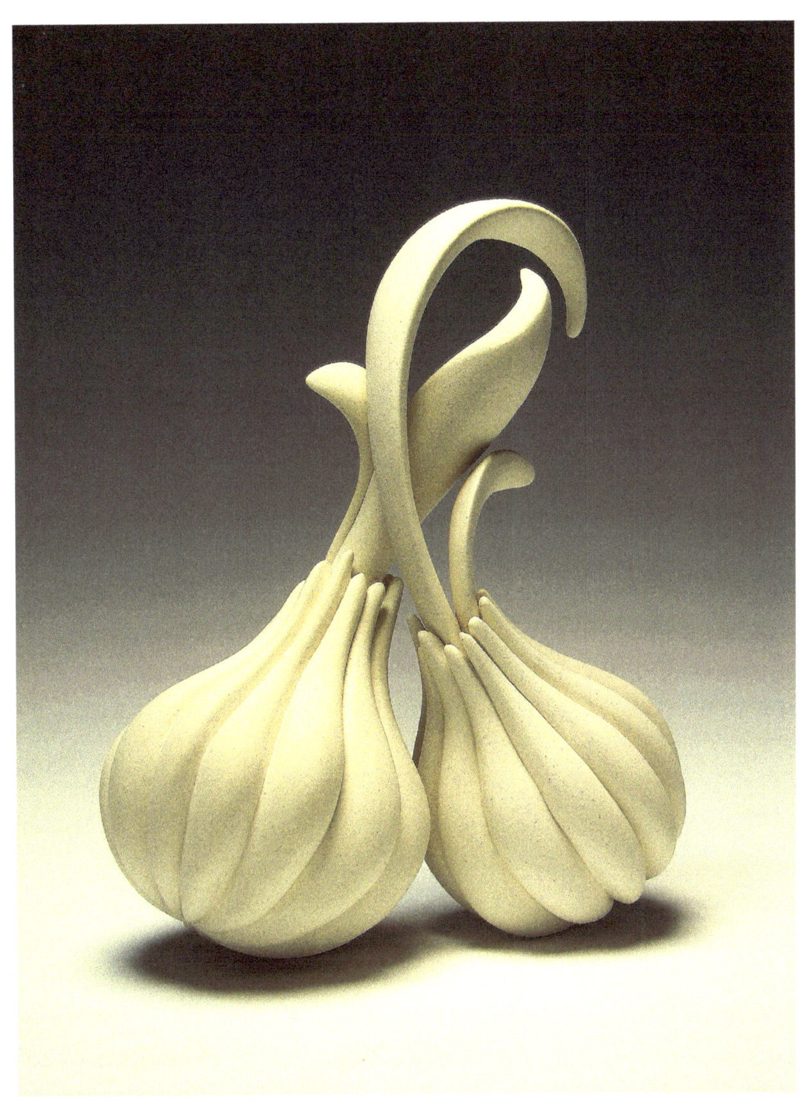

Katie White
Love Bulbs, 2012
Porcelain
7 x 5 x 4 Inches

Ecumene: Global Interface in American Ceramics invites us to investigate essential questions about the nature of creative action in the early 21st century. In computer science, *interface* refers to a point of interaction between components that allows them to function independently while communicating and working with other parts of a system. The range of ideas and approaches to clay working in this exhibition demonstrate that while this confluence of interconnectedness and independence is pervasive, it can also be discomforting. Artists influence culture, but what influences artists? Why and how do we create and what are the consequences of our work? Although it has been widely held that art has always shaped the culture around us, how can art serve as a vehicle for social criticism, reveal notions of identity or ways of living in empathy with the planet and its inhabitants?

The history of Academie Internationale de la Ceramique or International Academy of Ceramics roughly parallels that of the National Council on Education for the Ceramic Arts. Both organizations were founded in the 1960s as clay was becoming re-imagined as an artists' material, and its position in university-level programs was being reconsidered. Since this time, certain socio-political events have significantly influenced the re-configuration of this still relatively new creative landscape from the diverse expanse of human culture's most ancient and omnipresent art form.

The normalization of US relations with Eastern Europe and China that began in the 1970s opened new opportunities for direct artistic exchange with vast regions of the world that had previously been closed to those born in the 1950s and later. Infused with rich traditions in ceramics and other art forms, the first glimpses of these creative worlds opened the eyes and minds of those working in the US to the imaginative and expressive compulsion of artists creating in the shadow of economic hardship and socio-political repression. The subsequent rise of information technology has resulted in unprecedented access to art historical source material and other data, visual and otherwise. Electronic publishing, e-communications and social media have contributed to a sense that former physical and cultural divides can be spanned from one's home. Another major influence has resulted from an informal international community that is emerging through increased access to creative opportunities, cross-cultural residencies and study opportunities.

Traditionally ceramic arts have evinced the human capacity to create, transform, enjoy and improve the quality of life through the design and production of durable, useful and beautiful objects. Several works in the exhibition remain fully committed to pursuits of beauty, craftsmanship and personal expression as ends in themselves. Their realization of global interface transpires through absorption and reconciliation of culturally diverse traditions with contemporary artistic influences to create something heretofore unseen. Others demonstrate the degree to which artistic action has shifted in the contemporary era to also address the impact our works can make on society and the mind. Another notable trend is the extent to which notions of identity are being constructed by reconsideration of what it means to be human within the context of the endangered eco-system that is the world we know today. Unlike earlier conceptions of identity, this one is both trans-national and trans-cultural.

NCECA is honored by the invitation to develop this exhibition in conjunction with the IAC's General Assembly. The current year of NCECA's exhibitions efforts has been generously supported by the National Endowment for the Arts, a federal agency. NCECA is also indebted for the graciousness of Santa Fe Community College in hosting this exhibition and grateful for the diligence, expertise and sensitivity of Gallery Director Clark Baughan and Ceramics Head James Marshall for acting along with Jane Sauer and NCECA Exhibitions Director Linda Ganstrom to conceptualize, select and stage the exhibition. The exhibition itself would not have been possible if not for the creative energy and ideas of the artists, both all those who submitted works for consideration and those fortunate enough to have their work selected. This project would not have been realized without the dedication and creative support of NCECA's staff, especially Special Projects Manager Kate Vorhaus and Communications Manager Candice Finn.

Thanks to all for bringing *Ecumene: Global Interface in American Ceramics* into being.

Patsy Cox, President
Joshua Green, Executive Director, NCECA

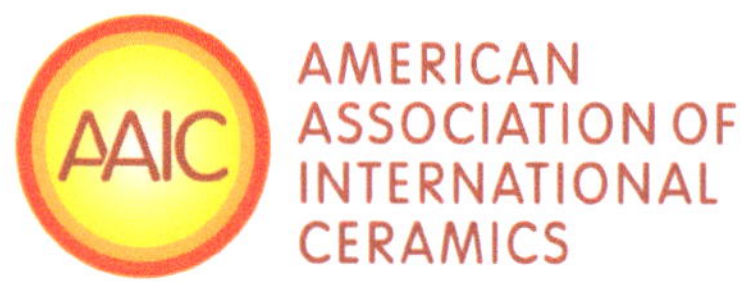

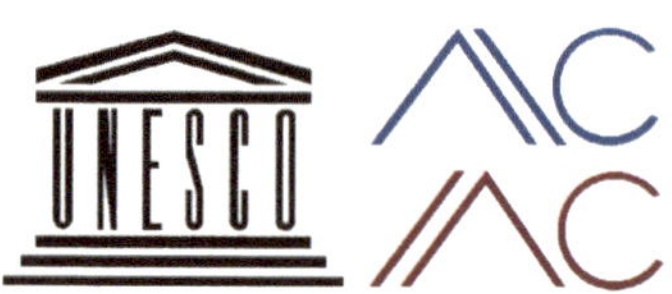

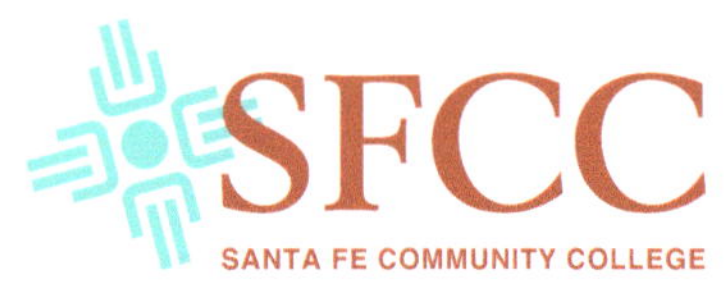

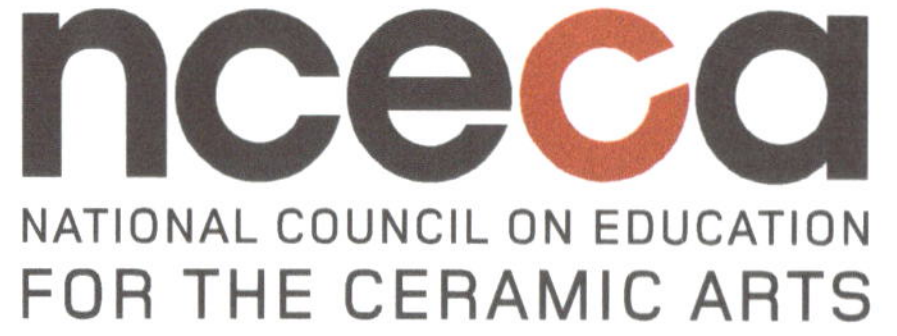

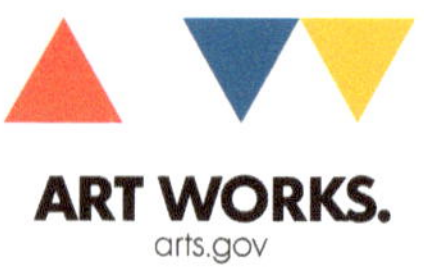

Back cover: Shalene Valenzuela, *Follow the Pattern: Let's Play Telephone,* 2012, Porcelain, underglaze illustration print transfer, 17 x 16 x 2 Inches

www.ingramcontent.com/pod-product-compliance
Ingram Content Group UK Ltd.
Pitfield, Milton Keynes, MK11 3LW, UK
UKHW060111300726

14090UKWH00002B/129

9781935046523